Come *to* ᴏᴜʀ Table

Come *to* our Table

A Midday Connection Cookbook

MELINDA SCHMIDT AND ANITA LUSTREA, EDITORS

NORTHFIELD PUBLISHING
CHICAGO

Scripture quotations marked NIV are taken from the Holy Bible, New International Version®. NIV®. Copyright © 1973, 1978, 1984 by International Bible Society. Used by permission of Zondervan. All rights reserved.

Scripture quotations marked THE MESSAGE are from The Message, copyright © by Eugene H. Peterson 1993, 1994, 1995. Used by permission of NavPress Publishing Group.

Cover & Interior Design: Julia Ryan | www.DesignByJulia.com
Images: ©JupiterImages.com

Thanks to Lori Neff, producer of *Midday Connection*, for her immeasurable assistance, and to Cheryl Dunlop, for her editorial preparation.

Library of Congress Cataloging-in-Publication Data

Come to our table : a Midday Connection cookbook / Melinda Schmidt and Anita Lustrea, editors.
    p. cm.
   Cookbook with recipes contributed from guests, staff, and listeners of the radio show Midday Connection from the Moody Broadcasting Network.
   Includes index.

 ISBN-13: 978-1-881273-90-5
 1. Cookery. I. Schmidt, Melinda. II. Lustrea, Anita. III. Midday connection (Radio program)
 TX714.C6253 2007
 641.5--dc22
                        2007025787

                   ISBN: 1-881273-90-3
               ISBN-13: 978-1-881273-90-5

We hope you enjoy this book from Northfield Publishing. Our goal is to provide high-quality, thought-provoking books and products that connect truth to your real needs and challenges. For more information on other books and products written and produced from a biblical perspective, go to www.moodypublishers.com or write to:

Northfield Publishing
215 West Locust Street
Chicago, IL 60610

1 3 5 7 9 10 8 6 4 2

Printed in the United States of America

Contents

Introduction

Welcome to our table! Pull up a chair. The Midday Connection community is getting ready to eat. We have lots of space at our table, and we hope you'll join us for a meal or two.

I don't know what "the table" signifies for you, but at our table you're going to experience family, warmth, community, learning, and growth.

What was the table like for you growing up? I grew up in a pastor's home where there was always room for one more at the table. I've been at the table with missionaries learning how God works in faraway places. I've spent time around the table with family where I've laughed so hard I've literally fallen off my chair. I've sat across the table having tea with close friends when the conversation was hard and painful situations were disclosed. Around the table is where strangers become friends.

Our invitation to the table allows you to sit alongside some of Midday Connection's favorite guests, who will share some of their best memories of the table. We'll also hear from some of our most loyal and involved listeners, as well as our Midday Connection and Moody Radio staff.

Of course the ultimate experience of the table is when we come together in community around the table of the Lord. This is the model for all of our other table experiences. It's our prayer at Midday Connection that you will continue to come to the table to learn and grow, and that you will open up your table to more and more people as a true reflection of our Lord's table.

May you have a continual feast of food and friendship at your table!

Anita Lustrea
Host & Executive Producer
Midday Connection

Get the Best Sermons by the World's Great Preachers

—only one of the inspiring features every week in the CHRISTIAN HERALD, which a prominent contemporary recently referred to as "the strongest interdenominational religious weekly in our country."

The Christian Herald

A Favorite Family Paper Since 1878

is throbbing with interest, for it believes in practical Christianity—something to LIVE here and now, to meet our everyday problems pressing for solution, to conquer wrongs, to alleviate suffering and to add to the sum of human happiness. Issued every week —52 times a year—for all denominations. Contributors include Margaret Slattery, Margaret E. Sangster, Wm. T. Ellis, LL.D., Sherwood Eddy, Wm. Jennings Bryan, Dr. Samuel D. Price, Bishop Wm. T. Manning, Rev. Wm. (Billy) Sunday, Dr. J. H. Jowett, Rev. D. J. Burrell, Rev. Paul Rader, Senator Arthur Capper, Wm. G. Shepherd, Wm. E. (Pussyfoot) Johnson, Dr. Charles M. Sheldon, etc. Price alone $2.00 a year.

MONEY SAVING COMBINATIONS

Independent (26 issues)	$3.00	BOTH FOR $4.00
Christian Herald (52 issues)	$2.00	SAVES $1.00

Independent Review of Reviews Christian Herald	All 3 $7.00	Independent Inter-Weekly Christian Herald	All 3 $5.50
American Independent Christian Herald	All 3 $6.50	Christian-Herald Independent Modern Priscilla	All 3 $5.50

Send Money Order or Check to
THE INDEPENDENT

140 Nassau Street   New York, N. Y.

P. S. Postage extra on Canadian and Foreign orders

SAVO FLOWER AND PLANT BOX

Self-Watering and Sub-Irrigating **For Windows, Porches, Sun Parlors, Etc.**

The All Year Round Garden

Leak-proof and rust-proof. You can move Savo Steel Boxes indoors or out and have beautiful Flowers and Plants the year around. Write for Free Catalog.

SAVO MFG. CO., Dept. "D," 39 So. La Salle St., Chicago, Illinois

---

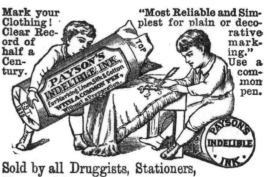

Appetizers

Recipes from MBN Staff

ELSA MAZON AND KELLEY PENA
producers of Prime Time America

This recipe is easy, fun to make, delicious, and international. It's also quick, inexpensive, and all-natural. Perfect for today's family at dinnertime, to enjoy with your small group or Bible study, or to take out on a picnic with your husband and kids.

Prime Time Guacamole

3 ripe avocados
1 vine ripe tomato, diced
½ small onion, minced
1 T fresh cilantro, chopped
1 T fresh lime juice
1 clove garlic, minced and mashed
1 fresh jalapeño, minced (remove seeds!)
salt to taste, about ½ tsp.
cayenne to taste

Cut avocados in half and scoop flesh into a bowl. Add remaining ingredients and stir till well combined. Serve with your favorite chips and enjoy!

NANCY TURNER
on-air host for WMBI-FM

I love to serve this appetizer. It makes me feel like I am eating food that is healthy, with whole and natural ingredients and the added benefit that it is quite satisfying. Plus, anytime an appetizer like this is served, everyone has to kind of get in a circle to reach it, and how beautiful it is to look at all the faces of people I love. It's a whole love feast thing!

Mediterranean Hummus Dip

1 container of plain hummus (whatever size you would like)
roasted marinated tomatoes in oil
pine nuts (toast them if you wish)

Empty the contents of the hummus onto a serving plate, then spoon as much of the tomatoes onto the top of the hummus as you would like, and next sprinkle pine nuts over it. Surround the dip with assorted crackers, baked pita chips, or vegetables such as celery, sugar snap peas, etc. Get creative with it!

Recipes from Midday Connection Listeners

RITA M. BEEDY
Urbana, OH—WEEC

This recipe is a family favorite! Many years ago my stepsister's dad married my mom, and one of the 5 sisters especially took us into her heart. Her name is Marcy, and she taught me a lot of things, like cooking, canning, crocheting, etc. This is one of the recipes she taught me.

Vegetable Dip

1 8 oz. package cream cheese, softened
2 chicken bouillon cubes
¼ cup hot water
1–2 T dried minced onions, to taste

Melt chicken bouillon cubes in hot water, then cool. Add to cream cheese and stir in minced onions. Blend well, chill, and serve with your favorite vegetables. Very simple, easy to double, and the ingredients are easy to find. Low-fat cream cheese can be used to lessen calories.

DARLENE DYKSTRA
Jenison, MI—WGNB

This recipe takes only about 15 minutes to prepare, and most of the ingredients are on hand. This is a great salsa that will have your guests always asking for the recipe!

Darlene's Salsa

2 cans (14½ oz.) diced, stewed, or crushed
    tomatoes (or you can use 4–5 large fresh
    tomatoes when in season)
2–3 bunches green onions
2 T jalapeño peppers (according to intensity desired)
2 T juice from the jalapeño peppers jar
    (again, according to intensity desired)
1 tsp. salt
3–4 T fresh cilantro
juice of 1–2 fresh limes
1–2 sweet and tart apples, peeled (preferably
    Granny Smith, Empire, or MacIntosh)

Place all ingredients into a food processor or blender and mix well. Best if you let it set for a couple of hours to let the flavors blend. This is also a wonderful side for roast beef.

Note: ½ cup sweetened tart cherries or dried sweetened cherries can be substituted for the apples or added to them.

CECELIA KENNEY
Hobart, IN—WMBI

I have made the recipe since the mid 1970s; it is one of my two specialty dishes that family and friends ask me to bring to gatherings. I gave a recipe to my daughter and daughters-in-law, and it has been passed on to their friends.

Some children will try, but all the adults will rave. I do have to tell strangers that it is not guacamole, because it looks similar.

Veggie Dip

Need blender; best if made a day ahead for blending of flavors.

½ cup real mayonnaise
5 or 6 green onions (tops and all), cleaned
¼ bunch fresh curly parsley
1 small clove garlic, clean and cut into pieces
pinch of salt

Mix in blender until creamy. Serve with fresh produce, cut into bite-sized pieces to prevent double dipping: green beans, carrots, celery, broccoli, cauliflower, cucumbers, cherry tomatoes, etc.

ANN MCBEE
Hagerstown, MD—WCRH

Ham Balls

1¼ lb. ham
1 lb. lean pork
½ lb. ground chuck
2 eggs
1½ cup saltine cracker crumbs (approx. 30 crackers)
1 cup milk

Have store grind meats together at time of purchase. Mix the ingredients well. Shape into 24 balls and place in shallow baking dishes. Mix sauce ingredients well and pour over balls before baking.

Sauce

2 cans tomato soup (undiluted)
1 cup vinegar
2¼ cups brown sugar
2 tsp. dry mustard

Bake the whole batch at 350° for 50–60 minutes, turning the balls over halfway through cooking time. May freeze in pans covered tightly with foil. When ready to serve, thaw and bake at 350° covered for 30 minutes and uncovered for 20 minutes.

CANDICE MCCANN
Rochester, IL—WLUJ

As a child I remember my mom making these wonderful snacks with fresh cucumbers from the garden every summer. I thought everyone had this wonderful treat during the summer, but was later surprised to find this seems to be a "family secret." Kid-friendly, quick, and inexpensive.

Nancy's Cucumber Boats

8 oz. cream cheese
½ cup real mayonnaise
2 tsp. minced fresh yellow or green onion
2 tsp. French dressing
6–8 medium cucumbers, peeled

Mix first 4 ingredients well and chill. Cut peeled cucumbers in half (lengthwise), remove seeds; then fill cucumber "boats" with chilled cream cheese mixture.

SHARRON MULDOON
Post Falls, ID—KMBI; I also teach English at the Moody Bible Institute campus in Spokane, WA

My family loves this recipe and it is a part of our holiday celebrations. I first got this recipe from a friend in 1974, the same year I became a Christian.

Party Cheese Ball

2 packages cream cheese, 8 oz. each
¼ pound crumpled Bleu cheese
½ pound extra-sharp cheddar cheese, grated
1 T Worcestershire sauce
½ tsp. cayenne pepper
½ tsp. seasoned salt
2 T grated onion
1 clove garlic, grated
1 cup chopped pecans (or walnuts)

Combine cheese in mixer bowl and beat until well blended. Add Worcestershire sauce, cayenne, seasoned salt, onion, garlic, and ½ cup of the chopped pecans. Shape into a ball or log and roll in remaining pecans. Chill thoroughly. Makes one large ball or two smaller balls or logs. Freeze if desired.

MURNA SLABAUGH
Sugarcreek, OH—WCRF

The first time I tasted these was at a Christmas tea the ladies from my church held. I was very surprised when I found what the ingredients were. I made these the first time for an extended family Christmas Eve celebration. The men in the family "snooted," but after they tried them, they went back for more! These are always a hit whenever I take them to a gathering.

Bacon Stuffed Dates

pitted dates
whole raw almonds
sliced bacon
maple or pancake syrup, thinned slightly
   with water

Soak toothpicks (one per date) in water for 1 hour. Cut each piece of bacon in half crosswise. Stuff each date with an almond, then wrap a piece of bacon around each date. Secure with a toothpick and set in a baking pan. When all dates have been stuffed and wrapped, brush with syrup. Bake at 400° for 15 or 20 minutes or until nicely browned. Drain on paper towels before serving. (Can be kept warm in Crock-Pot for serving.)

CATHY VROOM
Westmont, IL—WMBI & podcast

This is a quick and easy recipe I can make in a flash and bring to share with a group of people. The appetizer table is a great place to meet and greet people at parties that you may not normally talk to, which can lead to doorways of ministry to their lives. My take-along pretzels always create a buzz that I can use to further get to know a new person or find a way to bring Christ into people's lives just through simple conversation.

This is a quick and easy recipe using things on hand when a social event takes you by surprise and you're just not comfortable going empty-handed.

Take-Along Anywhere Pretzels

1 box or bag sourdough thick pretzels
1 bottle popcorn oil
1 packet French onion soup mix
1 tsp. garlic salt

Preheat oven to 350°. While pretzels are still in the bag, break them up into small bite-sized pieces. Spread pretzels onto cookie sheet. Mix together oil, salt, and soup mix—best if you mix in a large Pyrex measuring cup. Pour over pretzels. Bake for 10 minutes—just enough to toast the pretzels—do not overbake. Place in a decorative tin and take to your event.

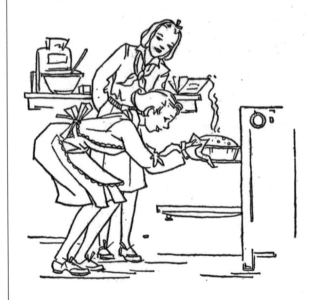

Main Dishes

SHARON HANBY-ROBIE
author of The Simple Home
www.sharonhanbyrobie.com

*Think this over carefully: The most charming
hours of our life are all connected—by a more or less
tangible hyphen—with a memory of the table.*
PIERRE-CHARLES MONSELET 1874

When I read the above quote I was immediately transformed to my childhood memories of sitting around the kitchen or dining room table. This is where life was lived. Meals at the kitchen table were boisterous, noisy, and often filled with laughter—occasionally to the dismay of my father. It wasn't often, but every once in a while Dad felt the need for a quiet dinner—a difficult challenge for our family of six children.

One evening in particular, Dad said, "The next person to laugh is going to bed without dinner!" At that moment, Mom lost it and burst out laughing as hard as she could. Of course, we all joined in laughing until we cried. Dad crumbled. And try as he might, he could not hold back the laughter as tears rolled down his face. It makes me sad to think how many families are missing out on the memory of family gathered together each evening for a meal.

Our dining room table was a multipurpose space. During the many family celebrations and get-togethers, this was where we came together. Having several generations gathered together at the table was an event in itself. I loved the discussions, both loud and soft, as we shared, learned, and simply lived together as family.

The dining room table was also the place where I cut my patterns for sewing and the freshly ironed clothes were placed for us to take to our rooms. It is where many homework projects were developed and refined. And most importantly to us children, it was where we played the weekend-long board games such as Monopoly. Now, as our family has continued to grow, it's exciting to watch as two new generations are joining in at the table for fun.

Chicken Paprikash

2 lbs. skinned chicken pieces
   (legs, breasts, and thighs)
½ cup flour
1½ tsp. salt
½ tsp. pepper
1 tsp. paprika
4 or 5 slices bacon
1 medium onion, chopped
½ green pepper, chopped
1 clove garlic, chopped
1 14 oz. can chicken broth
3 T flour
½ cup water
½ pint sour cream

Mix together in plastic bag flour, salt, pepper, and paprika. Coat chicken pieces by shaking in bag with flour mixture. Fry bacon in fryer; then remove from pan and reserve. Sauté onion, green pepper, and garlic until tender. Remove from pan. Brown chicken pieces in bacon grease; add a little olive oil if necessary. Remove from fryer. Pour leftover grease from fryer pan. Put chicken, green pepper, onion, garlic, and chicken broth in fryer pan. Cover and simmer 1–1½ hours until chicken is tender. Remove chicken from pan. Mix water with flour. Add to broth mixture in pan. Heat and stir until thickened. Then add sour cream and heat until smooth. Add crumbled bacon and return chicken to mixture. *Serve with spaetzels (recipe below).*

Spaetzels

2 cups flour
2 eggs
pinch of salt
½ cup water
¼ tsp. baking powder

Mix together, then drop into boiling water by ½ teaspoons. When all of the spaetzels have risen to the top of the water, they are done. Drain, add a tablespoon of butter, and serve.

NANCY KANE
author of From Fear to Love

I feel a bit nostalgic about this recipe as I have used it for more than 30 years (I date myself), and it has stood the test of time. This simple but elegant stroganoff recipe has marked the various seasons and passages of my life. It comes from the first recipe book I received as a gift when I was fresh out of college and living on my own. The extent of my cooking at that point was to boil water to make a box of macaroni and cheese, so a book of recipes was a welcome relief.

I tried this stroganoff recipe for the first time as a single, career-minded twenty-something when I entertained my boss and his wife for dinner. It was a hit when I served it as a young wife anxious to impress my folks for the first time in our new home. As the years went by and our children came, it was this beef stroganoff recipe that I relied on when I wanted to guarantee a meal my tiny discriminating eaters would enjoy. The recipe book is now worn and ragged, but the memories that it brings to mind remain fresh and vibrant and warm my heart with much gratitude.

Beef Stroganoff
Yield: 4–6 servings

2–2½ lbs. beef (high quality, tenderloin, sirloin)
3 T flour
½ tsp. salt
¼ tsp. pepper
3 T olive oil
3 onions, sliced thin
½ cup tomato juice
1 can Campbell's beef consommé
½ tsp. sugar
½ cup low-fat sour cream
½ lb. sliced mushrooms

Cut meat into thin strips. Toss in flour, salt, and pepper. Brown meat and onions in olive oil. Add tomato juice, consommé, and sugar. Reduce heat and simmer until meat is tender (be careful to not overcook meat). Blend in sour cream and mushrooms. Heat but do not boil. Serve over hot buttered noodles, with fresh green beans with sliced almonds, warm rolls, and mixed green salad.

GRAHAM AND TREENA KERR
authors of Recipe for Life
www.grahamkerr.com

Cooks from the beginning of recorded culinary history in both China and India have known how salt, sweet, sour, and bitter can be juggled together to create truly addictive sensations.

We have now reached a degree of "sophistication" in recipe development in which addictive levels of salt, fats, and sugars have been served up in enormous portions simply in order to gain or retain a share of today's consumer market.

Today's "food entrepreneurs" and blue-chip manufacturers are strongly motivated by enormous competitive pressure and are assisted by the most agile advertising and promotion industry that the world has ever seen.

Every single day we, the modern consumer, are urged to buy into some form of excess consumption, and we are promised that we will enjoy it and come back for more. By and large the promises are prophetic; we do return, we do eat more and more . . . and we are now suffering from self-inflicted wounds.

Scripture speaks of there being no temptation other than "what is common to man. And God is faithful; he will not let you be tempted beyond what you can bear" (1 Cor. 10:13).

My strong opinion is that the only message able to help us to stand up under the modern food marketing system is the gospel of Jesus Christ.

The Great Commandment really says it all. " 'Love the Lord your God with all your heart and with all your soul and with all your mind and with all your strength.' The second is this: 'Love your neighbor as yourself.' There is no commandment greater than these" (Mark 12:30–31).

This wasn't a suggestion . . . this was a commandment that embraced all the law and all the prophets.

So . . . what is our response as we now live out our generation in the gospel? We can love God for everything He has done and continues to do for us and, in the same spirit (without criticism or condemnation of anyone), we can lovingly share out of our abundance with our neighbors in need.

Tilapia Panfried in Bread Crumbs
Serves 2

**2 4 oz. tilapia fillets
2 T flour
1 egg
⅓ cup toasted plain bread crumbs
½ tsp. salt
¼ tsp. pepper
½ tsp. dill weed
olive oil spray
1 lemon**

Rinse fish and allow to come to room temperature. Measure flour, egg, and bread crumbs in three separate dishes (oblong plastic trays from the seafood department work well). Season the flour with salt, pepper, and dill weed. Beat the egg. Cut the lemon into wedges.

Preheat a heavy based skillet to medium high, 300°. Using a pair of tongs, dip the fillets back and front in the seasoned flour. Dip into the eggs to completely coat. Finally, flop the fillets into the bread crumbs. Use a spoon to ensure complete coverage. Spray the pan and both sides of the fish with olive oil.

Fry for 3 minutes; then turn for another 2 minutes. Internal temperature should reach 160°. Serve immediately with lemon wedges.

Baked Tilapia with Mushrooms and Spinach

Yield: 2 servings

6 1" white mushrooms
9 oz. tilapia fillets
olive oil spray
½ tsp. salt, divided
2 tsp. lemon juice
½ tsp. dill weed
2 cups tightly packed baby spinach leaves
¼ tsp. white pepper
¼ cup green onion, finely chopped
¼ tsp. herbs of provence
¼ tsp. salt
½ tsp. paprika

Preheat oven and baking dish to 425°. Slice mushrooms ¼" thick; include stalk. Wash tilapia in cold water and dry on paper towels.

Clean mushrooms with a soft brush and spray lightly with olive oil. Season with ¼ tsp. of the salt, lemon juice, and dill. It helps to do this on a plate. Spray spinach lightly with oil and season with ¼ tsp. of the salt and the white pepper. Set aside.

Heat a skillet to 200°. Toss in the mushrooms and green onions and fry for 2 minutes. Add sprayed, seasoned spinach and stir to just wilt the spinach. Remove to a plate to keep warm.

Spray the tilapia with oil and season with herbs and salt. Sear quickly in the hot skillet for 30 seconds on each side.

Transfer the mushroom spinach mixture to a baking dish, making 2 mounds. Top each with a seared tilapia filet, dust with paprika, spray with oil, and bake for 8 minutes (160° internal temperature).

Used by permission from *Day by Day Gourmet* (September 1, 2007, B & H Publishing Group).

Susie Martinez, Vanda Howell, and Bonnie Garcia
authors of Don't Panic, Dinner's in the Freezer

Keeping Others in Mind

Using the *Don't Panic* method, making meals ahead of time and freezing them, provides you with a creative way to help others by supplying them with a meal during stressful times. You will find that you always have a variety of meals available to pull out of your freezer and give to someone in need. Here are some examples of people who would appreciate your help.

- New moms
- Singles, especially single parents
- Those dealing with bad-day syndrome

- The elderly
- Those suffering from sickness or family death
- Stocking a community freezer

We all have friends, neighbors, and relatives who need our help on certain occasions. Although we have a genuine desire to help them, with today's busy schedules, it may be difficult to do so. The beauty of using the *Don't Panic* method of cooking is that it takes very little time, money, or energy to help those we care about in a substantial way. You can provide relief with a personal touch that will let them know you care.

Apricot-Glazed Chicken Tenders

Yield: 4–6 servings

2 lbs. chicken tenders, cut-up breast pieces, or chicken wings, tips removed

Marinade
**⅓ cup vegetable oil
3 cloves garlic, minced
2 T lemon juice
1 tsp. rosemary
1 tsp. thyme
salt and pepper to taste (approx. ¼ tsp.)
1 small bay leaf, crumbled**

In large freezer bag, combine marinade ingredients.

Apricot Glaze
**1 onion, minced
1 T unsalted butter
2 T cider vinegar
1 cup apricot preserves
1 T soy sauce
2 tsp. Dijon mustard
¼ tsp. ginger
¼ tsp. cloves
¼ tsp. salt
⅛ tsp. pepper**

In saucepan, cook onions in butter over moderate heat, stirring until softened. Add vinegar and continue cooking until liquid has reduced by one half. Add preserves, soy sauce, Dijon mustard, and spices. Cook uncovered, stirring occasionally, for 10 minutes or until thick. Place mixture in a food processor or blender and puree.

Cooking day instructions: Make marinade. Add chicken pieces to marinade, toss to coat, and marinate at room temperature one hour. Meanwhile, prepare the apricot glaze. After 1 hour of marinating time, freeze. (If preparing for that day, marinate chicken in fridge 6–8 hours or overnight. Prepare apricot glaze and refrigerate.)

Freeze apricot glaze in a separate, smaller freezer bag. Store in freezer together with marinated chicken.

Serving day instructions: Thaw chicken pieces and discard marinade. Place chicken on rack of broiler pan and broil 6 inches from heat, 5 minutes on each side. Baste chicken generously with apricot glaze and broil 3 minutes on each side or until well glazed and brown. Adjust cooking time if using thicker cuts of chicken.

Hint: Chicken can also be prepared on a charcoal or gas grill. To bake chicken, place pieces in a large baking dish. Bake at 425° for approximately 25–30 minutes, basting with apricot glaze and turning every 10 minutes. Do not overcook. Shortly before chicken is done, put the chicken under the broiler and broil until golden brown and bubbly.

Adapted from Susie Martinez, Vanda Howell, and Bonnie Garcia, *Don't Panic, Dinner's in the Freezer*, Fleming H. Revell, a division of Baker Publishing Group, 2005. Used by permission.

KATHY PEEL

author of The Family Manager Takes Charge *and* Be Your Best

www.familymanager.com

The Peel Family's Excellent Kitchen Adventures

For years, I gave cooking my best shot. I labored over cookbooks and food magazines, attempted new recipes, and tried different techniques. I got into nutrition in a big way, banning white sugar and refined flour from our home. I drove to a farm to buy honey straight from the hive, made my own peanut butter, and baked all our bread before realizing that I'd gone overboard—when it was really my bread that should have. It would have made the perfect anchor.

For a number of reasons, my family's health in particular, I decided to accept the truth about myself and give up trying to be a culinary diva. I was out of my depth, making myself and everyone else miserable and putting my children in a compromising position about truthfully being thankful at dinnertime. We decided to work together as a family to make the evening meal a more positive experience.

First off, we voted that Bill should cook whenever possible. He's better at it than I am. That way the boys didn't have to worry about their turkey burgers turning into turkey jerky. I did most of the grocery shopping and table decorating. The boys became on-call sous-chefs and assistant table setters.

We found that food and teamwork go hand in hand, perhaps more naturally than any other area of family management. Eating and cooking together build bonds. Even the youngest child can, with encouragement, participate in family conversations around the dinner table and carry flatware or dishes to or from the table, wash carrots (even if they have to be discreetly rewashed), or help stir the corn bread batter.

There's something about sitting down and eating together, especially when everybody has had a hand in getting the meal on the table, that promotes family bonding. And after a hard day, it's wonderful to eat dinner with people you love. Since I don't add much to the quality of the food at my home outside of a few dishes I've mastered, I see my most important role as initiating good conversation that brings out the best of the diners, whether they're my own family or guests we've invited to share our meal.

Chicken in the Blankets

This dish is a favorite for family get-togethers as well as dinner parties.

3–4 chicken breasts
salt, pepper, garlic, curry to taste
1 can crescent rolls
2 cans cream of chicken soup
1½ cups milk
1 cup grated cheddar cheese, divided

Stew chicken with salt, pepper, and garlic. Let cool, and then shred. Unroll and press out individual crescent rolls into triangles. Place a portion of shredded chicken in the middle of a flattened roll. Pull two bottom corners across to middle of the chicken, and roll up. Place each stuffed roll in a greased baking dish with top corner of triangle facing down.

Mix soup, milk, ½ cup cheese, and a dash of curry in a saucepan over low heat until blended together. Pour entire mixture over stuffed rolls. Sprinkle remaining cheese on top and bake for 40 to 45 minutes at 350°.

MARCIA RAMSLAND
speaker and author of Simplify Your Life *and* Simplify Your Space
www.OrganizingPro.com

What's for Dinner Tonight?

Did you know that most people cook the same three to five meals over and over? If you're in this same kind of a mealtime "rut," you're not alone.

The secret to breaking out of your mealtime habits is very simple. Take a pad of paper and pen to dinner tonight and announce, "I need a list of 14 meals that you like that I cook." Soon the family will be chiming in with a list of long-forgotten favorites and you'll be getting energized to cook again.

Post the list inside the cabinet with your dinner dishes. When you're faced with that daily question, "What's for dinner tonight?" you can casually open your cabinet and review your list. As you review the list for ingredients on hand, you can announce the dinner entrée to a cheering, hungry family or spouse.

Remember, the problem is not cooking the meal, but deciding what to cook and having the ingredients on hand. Plan your mealtimes and menus for the week ahead by checking your calendar on Sunday night. Jot down the weekend meals at the end of the week before going grocery shopping. With this weekly routine you'll simplify your mealtime stresses and enjoy cooking again.

Ten Time-Saving Tips for Meals

1. Begin with a clean kitchen.

2. Make sure the clean dishes are out of the dishwasher.

3. Set the table before cooking to motivate yourself to get dinner going.

4. Estimate how long it will take to get a meal ready, and then try to beat the clock.

5. Prepare the longest part of the meal first.

6. Decide what can be done while another dish is baking.

7. Avoid traffic jams at the kitchen sink by keeping your wastebasket out while cooking.

8. Place a stool nearby so the kids and guests can talk while dinner is being made.

9. Alert everyone five minutes before a meal so you can sit down together.

10. Remember, a good meal is more than the food. It's also about the mood, so be cheerful when you sit down together.

A Simple Prayer of Thanks

Dear God, thank You for the blessings of family and friends. Help my kitchen to become a place of refuge from the day and an encouragement for facing whatever life brings tomorrow. Fill our mealtimes with love and laughter. And help me to make changes that will make it fun to be at my house. Amen.

If you are organized and prepared, dinnertime will become more of a joy and less of a chore. You can do it. Bon appetit!

Excerpt used with permission from *Simplify Your Life* (Nashville: W Publishing, 2003).

Five Steps for a 15-Minute Meal Cleanup

Cleanup can be done faster than you think.

1. Clear the table and leave only the centerpiece. Load the dishwasher, collect hand-washed items, and put the leftovers away ASAP. Get the whole family involved to speed up the process. (Time: five minutes)

2. Set up a rotating family schedule for dishwashing. Wash the remaining pots and pans right after the meal before they get crusty and take twice as long to get done. (Time: five minutes)

3. Wipe off the table and the kitchen counters. (Time: one minute)

4. Put the dried dishes and the drying rack away as soon as possible. A kitchen always looks messy if dishes are continually drying on the counter. (Time: two minutes)

5. Empty the garbage and clean the floor as needed. (Time: two minutes)

Total time spent in cleanup: fifteen minutes. Now you're finished for the evening and can do something else you enjoy!

Excerpt used with permission from *Simplify Your Life* (Nashville: W Publishing, 2003).

Your Kitchen Table Sets the Tone

A clean kitchen table can set the tone for your entire home. It is one of the most used gathering spots and should be ready for action anytime.

A simple way to keep your kitchen table looking nice is to keep it cleared except for a tasteful centerpiece. Then it always looks nice whether you are walking by for a drink of water, helping the kids do their homework, or chatting with a neighbor over a cup of coffee. If you keep up on nothing else in your home, keep your kitchen table cleared off and something of interest, such as a silk flower arrangement, as a centerpiece.

Excerpt used with permission from *Simplify Your Space* (Nashville: Thomas Nelson, 2007).

I love to make something that is simple to make, but seems "elegant" to put on the table for company or family. This baked salmon recipe does it! You can bake it in 30 minutes while you cook rice and vegetables and set the table. Voila, the meal's ready and company dinner is served!

Baked Salmon

skinless salmon (1/3–1/2 lb. per serving)
butter
lemon juice
garlic salt with parsley

Choose a rectangular serving dish that fits inside a holder you can serve on the table. Rinse the salmon and place it in foil inside your ovenware serving dish. Daub with butter and lemon juice and top with garlic salt with parsley. Seal the foil tightly over the top of the salmon and the ends.

Bake at 350° for 30 minutes. Open foil and use a knife to see that the thickest part of the salmon is almost white. If it is still pink, cook for 5 minutes longer or until done. Roll back the foil, place the pan in the serving holder, and serve with rice and steamed vegetables. Sit back an enjoy the "ohs and ahs" of company at your table.

JANE RUBIETTA
author of Resting Place
www.abounding.org

The Foods We Treasure

In junior high, my friend often lunged off the bus with a "missing item" report. "I can't find my ring." "I lost my favorite bracelet." "My mom's dishcloth disappeared last night." We wondered in our adolescent way about these strange vanishings and headed off to history, gym class, or science.

One day, she declared, "Our basset hound got really sick yesterday. We rushed him to the vet, who opened up his stomach. Guess what we found?"

The poor dog's inventory included a ring, a bracelet, a dishcloth, and a pair of underwear. My stomach hurts to even imagine his diet. But sometimes, my diet isn't much better. I feed on worry or fear; I feast on regret; I gobble up resentment; I regurgitate unforgiveness. St. John of the Cross said, "We are diminished by the trivial things we treasure."

Our treasures show up in our stomach, our soul. We eat from the wrong table. How sound is our nutritional plan? And what do we really believe about God? He is able to fill us with good (Luke 1:53), with all the fullness of Christ (Eph. 3:19), with the Spirit (Eph. 5:18), with knowledge (Col. 1:9), with joy (2 Tim. 1:4), with the fruit of righteousness (Phil. 1:11). And when Jesus says, "Blessed are you who hunger now, for you will be satisfied" (Luke 6:21), the root word for *satisfied* leans toward supplying food in abundance, from the word for *gorge*.

Job 36:16 says, "He is wooing you from the jaws of distress to a spacious place free from restriction, to the comfort of your table laden with choice food." Today, may God woo us to that spacious place, to that table, laden with abundance: love, goodness, grace, kindness, forgiveness. And may we be filled to overflowing.

Fast and Fabulous Bleu Cheese Chicken

12-oz. jar Marie's or T. Marzetti's bleu cheese dressing
2–3 pounds boneless, skinless chicken breasts

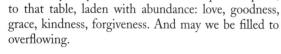

Preheat oven to 350°. Spray 9x12" casserole dish with nonstick cooking spray. Slice chicken breasts butterfly-style and place in bottom of dish. Cover with bleu cheese dressing. Bake for 45 minutes until bubbly and slightly golden on top. Serve with steaming brown rice.

This has become a standard company dish—it looks and tastes delicious but takes minutes to prepare, and thus it allows me freedom to ready my heart for our friends rather than fret over food. Even our children's friends love it, wanting the recipe to take to their mothers. I always want to supervise kitchen cleanup for this dish, because the dark crisp stuff on the sides of the dish is the best part!

Jan Silvious
author of Moving Beyond the Myths
and Look at It This Way
www.jansilvious.com

Boy Food

At our house, dinnertime was important. Over the years, my husband, Charlie, had "come home" times anywhere from 4:30 to 6:00. It was the unspoken rule at our house that when Daddy comes home, we have dinner. I liked it that way, even if on some days I fixed a really quick meal because the boys and I had been out doing our thing. Having a set mealtime (when Daddy gets home) gave stability and strong parameters to our family life. Looking back over the years, I know that is one thing we did so right! I am grateful for the memories and for the fun we had around the dinner table. It is still one of our favorite places to gather and reminisce. Of course, now it doesn't depend on when Daddy gets home. Now, the gathering happens when the boys get home!

Our home was a place where "boy food" was supreme. Calico Beans was a favorite recipe. Our sons ate them heartily when they were first prepared, and they loved to have them in the refrigerator as leftovers. To this day, if my boys and their families are coming for a day of swimming and casual food, I know Calico Beans will be a hit. They are easy to prepare and always great to eat!

Calico Beans

1 lb. turkey bacon, cooked crisp and crumbled
1 small onion, chopped and sautéed
1 16 oz. can lima beans
1 16 oz. can pork and beans
1 16 oz. can pinto beans
1 16 oz. can small kidney beans
3 T brown sugar
3 T white sugar
2 T yellow mustard
2 T Worcestershire sauce
1 lb. cheddar cheese cut in cubes

Combine all ingredients (except cheese), including juice from cans of beans, in a Crock-Pot. Cook on low all day. About two hours before you plan to serve, add cheese cubes to beans and stir. The cheese makes a wonderful, creamy touch to the whole dish.

If you have a good recipe for jalapeño corn bread, mix it up and serve hot with these beans. This is definitely a "boys and men" meal.

Recipes from MBN Staff

Marie Bailey
administrative assistant, MBN

*This recipe is **very** easy. You can put it together the night before you eat it and let it cook all night! This recipe was given to me by my best friend of 36 years. In high school we double-dated to the Christmas ball. Instead of going out to dinner, we decided to cook dinner for the guys. Holly and I had such fun that day: hair in rollers, nervous about the ball, getting dressed up before dinner. Holly and I are still friends and I'm still making this recipe. Every time I do, it brings a smile to my face as I remember that night and special friends.*

Crock-Pot Roast

beef pot roast
1 or 2 cans cream of mushroom soup
1 or 2 packets Lipton onion soup mix

Place both kinds of soup in a bowl and mix well. (The size of the pot roast and how much gravy you want will determine if you use 1 or 2 cans of mushroom soup and packets of onion soup mix.) Leftovers can be used later to make hot beef sandwiches.

Spoon half of soup mixture on the bottom of the Crock-Pot. Place pot roast on top of soup mixture. Spoon remaining soup mixture on top of pot roast. Turn Crock-Pot on low and let cook overnight. The soup mixture makes its own gravy while cooking. If it's too thick, add a bit of water to thin out before serving. Serve with mashed potatoes and any other vegetables you want.

BETH BATEMAN
New Windsor, IL
office administrator and
promotions director of WDLM

Here is my grandmother's recipe for ham balls. As soon as we walked into her house, we could smell the aroma from this dish. It is delicious and simple to make. When we make it now, it reminds us of how she would feed our bodies with great food and feed us spiritually by teaching us about love and devotion for our Lord.

Ham Balls

Yield: 6–8 servings

1½ lbs. ground ham
1 lb. ground beef
2 cups bread crumbs
2 eggs
1 cup milk
1 cup brown sugar
½ cup water
½ cup vinegar
1 tsp. dry mustard

Combine ham, beef, bread crumbs, eggs, and milk in a large bowl. Form mixture into balls and place in a pan or baking dish. In a separate bowl, mix brown sugar, water, vinegar, and dry mustard. Pour this mixture over meatballs and bake uncovered at 325°. Bake for 1 hour.

TRICIA BOYLE
program producer for MBN

Pepperoni spaghetti is one of my favorite dishes that my mom makes (and now I make). It was always my choice for my birthday meal. She still makes it when I visit over the holidays. It's a great make-ahead casserole, and the leftovers reheat well too.

The second recipe, pizza grinders, is a great hands-on recipe for kids and teens, as well as adults—and wonderful for picky eaters because individuals can make it how they like it. My family has been making this for more than 15 years, and we love introducing new people to this unique meal!

Pepperoni Spaghetti

6 oz. spaghetti
optional: 2 slices onion, chopped
tomato sauce (2 8 oz. cans)
½ tsp. oregano
½ tsp. basil
1 pkg. sliced Swiss cheese (8 slices)
1 lb. shredded mozzarella
pepperoni slices

Cook spaghetti according to directions. While spaghetti is cooking, heat tomato sauce, oregano, basil. If adding onion, sauté a couple slices of chopped onion in ¼ cup melted margarine. Add onion to the tomato sauce mixture. Grease casserole dish (either 8x10" or 8x8").

Layer the following two times: pepperoni slices (side by side, covering the area of pan) and ½ of sauce mixture, ½ of spaghetti (cooked and drained), ½ of cheese (Swiss then mozzarella).

Bake uncovered in casserole dish at 350° for 30 minutes or until cheese is bubbling.

Pizza Grinders

frozen bread dough loaves
pizza sauce
mozzarella cheese
assorted pizza toppings

Thaw dough for 2–3 hours. Cut into thirds or fourths. Flatten each section of dough and fill with sauce, cheese, and toppings, making sure to leave at least ½ inch around the edges. Fold edges over and secure with toothpicks. (You can identify yours with a piece of pepperoni or an olive on top.) Lightly grease the cookie sheet(s) or spray with cooking spray to keep from sticking. Bake for 30 minutes at 350°.

Joe Carlson
producer, MBN

I made this when I was a bachelor. When I had people over they were surprised at how good this dish was—and that I had made it!

Chicken Rice-A-Roni Thing

2 boxes Rice-A-Roni
3 chicken breasts
1 can peas or 1 bag small frozen peas
handful of cashews
soy sauce to taste

Cook Rice-A-Roni according to directions. Chop chicken into 1-inch cubes. When adding water to Rice-A-Roni, add uncooked chicken. Continue according to Rice-A-Roni directions. Add peas and warm through. Serve with some soy sauce and sprinkle with cashews. (Don't mix cashews in while everything is cooking, though—they will get soft.)

Annette DiMarco
office administrator, WKES
St. Petersburg, FL

Sausage cacciatore was always a winter comfort food in our Northern household. When I was coming home from school and entering our hallway, the aroma from my mom's cooking would quicken my steps up 3 floors to our apartment. This is a main dish that can be served by itself or over rice or spaghetti.

The second recipe, spiedini, is wonderful for a buffet or as an appetizer. You can also make the pieces large enough to be added and cooked in your Italian tomato sauce. It would then be called Bracciole with the added ingredients of a sliced hard-boiled egg and salami. It was a family joke that our dad would yell to my sister and me, "What's Mommy making today?" We would scream back, "Bracciole!" I think we just liked to say the word.

Sausage Cacciatore

12 Italian sausage links
1 green pepper
1 large chopped onion
½ jar kalamata olives, chopped
1 can mushrooms
extra virgin olive oil
2 cans whole tomatoes
pinch of sugar
salt and pepper to taste

Place sausage in a saucepan and cover the top of the sausage with water. Simmer on medium heat. Prick sausage to allow fat to escape. Skim top of water for fat. When sausage turns gray and water is gone, continue to let sausage brown. After browning, cut into 1-inch pieces and set aside.

Brown green pepper, onions, olives, and mushrooms in olive oil. Add sausage pieces to mixture. Shred tomatoes in blender and strain for seeds, and add to mixture. Add sugar, salt, and pepper.

Transfer to baking dish and bake at 375° until sauce thickens.

Spiedini

2½ to 3 lbs. sirloin tip or bottom round
bread crumbs
grated Parmesan cheese
onion
tomato
extra-virgin olive oil
salt and pepper

Pound out your meat using a mallet to make it thin and tender. Cut into 2-inch strips.

Mix bread crumbs, cheese, and onion with oil to moisten mixture. Add salt and pepper to taste. (This mixture is not measured. Do it to your taste.) Cut tomatoes into small pieces (as you would for a taco).

Set aside a plate of oil. Take each strip of meat and dip in oil; take a spoonful of bread crumb mixture and a piece of tomato and place in center of meat strip. Roll up and secure with toothpicks. Broil.

Tip: When my mother taught me to make this recipe she said, "You **broil** when you dip in **oil**. You **bake** when you dip in **egg**." These meat strips can be coated in egg and rolled in the leftover bread crumb mixture, then baked at 350° till brown. Yummy!

JENNIFER HAYDEN EPPERSON
station manager of WRMB

This was the last meal that my lovely mother, Betty Hayden, prepared for me and my husband when she visited my new home in Florida. Two months later the Lord took her home. I sure miss Mom and her cooking! Quick and easy!

Steak Supper in a Foil Package

1½ lbs. chuck steak (1-inch thick)
1 can (10½ oz.) cream of mushroom soup
1 envelope (1½ oz.) dry onion soup mix
3 medium carrots, cut into ½-inch pieces
2 stalks of celery, cut into 1-inch pieces
3 medium potatoes, pared and quartered
2 T water

Heat oven to 450°. Place 24x18" piece of heavy aluminum foil in baking pan. Place meat on foil. Stir mushroom soup and onion soup mix and spread over meat. Top with vegetables. Sprinkle water over vegetables. Fold foil over and seal securely. Cook 1½ hours or until tender.

JON GAUGER
*special project producer for MBN
and on-air talent*

When our daughter announced her engagement, we made plans to host a cookout for her future in-laws. Feeling inadequate at my grilling skills (and nervous because we wanted to make a good impression), I started getting desperate. Then a clandestine idea began to take shape. We were invited to a function at Lynnette's future brother-in-law's where the grill was fired up. I decided to carefully watch every single step in the process this grill master used—and copy him. To my surprise, his big "secret" was dumping the meat into a Ziploc bag with Wishbone Italian dressing. That's it! No basting on the grill. No special tricks of any kind.

I copied him exactly. When our new in-laws arrived, they were truly impressed. My daughter's future father-in-law said to me, "I don't know what your secret is, but you and one of my sons ought to get together for a cook-off." I confessed everything—and the wedding went beautifully.

Super-Easy Marinade

Place meat (chicken, beef, anything) in gallon-size Ziploc bag. Generously add Wishbone Italian dressing to cover. Let stand at least 2 hours in the fridge— overnight is better. Before placing on grill, thoroughly coat with dressing. Grill meat to perfection and get ready for lots of compliments!

JOE LUNDBERG
meteorologist for WMBI mornings

"I stumbled onto this recipe one day at a restaurant I worked at. It was very warm to the taste and much meatier than anything my mom had ever made. I found the recipe, adjusted it so that it would fit into a Crock-Pot, and I've helped warm many a tummy ever since!"

Lundberg's Steak Loft Chili

2 lbs. ground meat
2 green peppers
1 large onion
1 28 oz. can crushed tomatoes
1½ bottles of chili sauce (approx. 18 oz.)
1 T chili powder
½ T crushed red pepper
½ T cayenne pepper
½ T cumin
3 or 4 bay leaves
1 16 oz. can kidney beans

Cook meat until brown. Drain off the grease. Place meat into a Crock-Pot, or any other suitable cooking bowl that is large enough. Dice the peppers and the onion, sauté them; then add in all of the other ingredients. Turn Crock-Pot on low, cover, and cook overnight, stirring occasionally. You can cook it faster if you wish. Just be careful to stir more frequently.

Serve as you like it. Oyster crackers or saltines are nice, but some serve with cheese melted on top with onions added for extra flavor. Yum! Tasty.

JAN MARKOWITZ
part of the Morning Team at WCRF, Cleveland, OH

This recipe has been in my husband's family for generations and was given to me by my wonderful, sweet mother-in-law.

Chicken Paprikash with Homemade Dumplings

1 cut-up chicken
1 chicken bouillon cube
1 cup sour cream
1 medium onion
1 tsp. diced paprika (or to taste)
2 T flour
1 pkg. chicken gravy

Brown chicken on both sides in broiler. Sprinkle with paprika and pepper. While chicken is browning, prepare gravy. Sauté onion in butter, add paprika after onion softens, then add dry chicken gravy mix and flour.

Cook for about 1 minute and then gradually add 3 to 4 cups of water. Add bouillon cube, constantly stirring so as not to get lumpy. You can adjust to desired thickness. Add more flour if you want a thicker gravy.

When chicken has browned on both sides in the broiler, allow to cool, break apart, and add to the gravy mixture. Cover and cook for 1 hour on top of the stove. Then remove some gravy from the pot and slowly add the sour cream. Return to pot and mix thoroughly. Juices that are left in the broiler from the chicken can be added to the gravy as well.

Dumplings

4 eggs
3 cups flour
1 cup sour cream
1½ tsp. salt

Mix together all ingredients, and drop by teaspoon into salted boiling water. Only takes about a minute once all dumplings have been added. Drain and pour chicken gravy over dumplings when ready to serve.

LORI NEFF
Midday Connection producer

My husband is a bit of a picky eater, so it can be a challenge to find things that he likes. Soon after we were married, I adapted this recipe that I found in a magazine to include things he likes and took out the things he doesn't like. He likes pretty much anything with cheddar cheese and chili. It's quick and super easy, but can look a little fancy.

Chili and Cheese-Stuffed Shells

1 can beef chili (we use the kind without beans, but you could use any variety)
1 egg, beaten
1 cup ricotta cheese
1 cup cheddar cheese
10 large pasta shells

Preheat oven to 350°. Put some water on to boil the pasta shells. Put the chili in a skillet to warm up. I usually sneak in some garlic and onion (the dried, minced kind) to give it something extra while the chili warms up. Meanwhile, in a medium bowl mix the egg, ricotta, and ½ cup cheddar. Cook the pasta for 5 minutes, then drain.

Place half of the warm chili mixture in a greased square pan (about 9"). After the pasta has cooled a bit, spoon some of the egg/cheese mixture into each and place on the chili. After filling all of the shells, cover with the remaining chili mixture. Cover with remaining cheese.

Bake until the cheese is melted and everything is heated through—about 30 minutes.

Serves 2–3. (Usually we'll each have a serving and then one of us will take the leftovers to work the next day for lunch.)

Note: The original recipe called for manicotti shells. You could use those instead, if you prefer—I just found these easier to handle.

Also, this recipe is very easy to double—just put everything in a 9x13" pan instead.

MELINDA SCHMIDT
Midday Connection host

Chicken a l'Indienne

1 large onion, chopped
2½ tsp. curry powder
2 T flour
1½ cup half-and-half
½ cup chicken broth (or 1 chicken bouillon cube
   in ½ cup hot water)
1 small (6 oz.) can tomato paste
3–4 uncooked skinless, boneless chicken breasts,
   diced into 1½-inch cubes

I make this on the stovetop in a Dutch oven. Brown onion in butter. Add flour and curry, and mix together. Add half-and-half, broth, and paste, and mix together. Add chicken. Cover and cook on medium-low 20–30 minutes, or until chicken is done, and serve over hot rice.

KELLI THOMPSON
Anderson/Indianapolis, IN
WGNR-FM morning host

This dish is a family favorite. It is delicious, easy, in-expensive, and can be made quite heart-healthy depending on your choice of ingredients.

Peach Picante Chicken

1 pound skinless breast meat chicken tenders
1 T olive oil
1 packet taco seasoning (choose low sodium for
   heart health!)
1 medium jar salsa or picante
1 small jar peach preserves
1 box instant rice (choose brown rice as a
   healthy option!)

Rinse chicken tenders in cool water, pat dry, and cut into bite-sized pieces. Toss chicken in taco seasoning, coating pieces on both sides. Brown the chicken in skillet with 1 T olive oil, turning so as to brown both sides. After tenders pieces are browned, add full jar of salsa or picante, cover, and simmer over low heat until chicken is cooked through, about 30 minutes. Occasionally stir.

After chicken is cooked through, add small jar of peach preserves to taste. (I usually add the full jar if it is 12 ounce size or smaller.) Stir until preserves are thoroughly mixed with salsa and chicken. Increase heat to medium-low and prepare enough rice according to box directions to serve 2 to 4 people.

When rice is ready, spoon onto serving plate and cover generously with Peach Picante Chicken mixture. This dish will be both mildly spicy and semisweet. It is best served with a side salad and iced tea. *Enjoy!*

Recipes from Midday
Connection Listeners

JANE AHRENS
Elmhurst, IL—WMBI

This is a popular dish at our church potlucks, and I have often been asked for the recipe. It is very easy to prepare, and I keep the ingredients on hand to make when I am in a hurry. I have substituted fat-free sour cream and reduced-fat cream of chicken soup to lower the fat content of the casserole.

Sour Cream Enchilada Casserole

Yield: 4-6 servings

2 10½ oz. cans cream of chicken soup
1 pint sour cream
1 4½ oz. can chopped green chilies
2 cups grated cheddar cheese
1 pkg. 6-inch flour tortillas (cut into 1-inch
   squares)
1 6½ oz. can sliced ripe olives

Mix all ingredients except tortillas. Add tortillas and mix until coated. Place in greased 9x13" pan or 3-quart casserole dish. Bake at 350° for 30 minutes.

SHARON ALDRICH
Fort Myers, FL—WSOR

After my husband had two stents put into his heart blood vessels and was told that he had high cholesterol, I had to change my "down-home Southern cooking" ways. We love fish, so I cooked it and spinach in a new way. This is a quick meal for busy people.

Sautéed Fish with Tender Crisp Spinach

2 mild fish fillets (Try to use fresh, but frozen defrosted may be substituted.)
4 T light (mild) olive oil, divided
lemon juice
1 small shallot, chopped finely
1 clove garlic, minced
1 lb. baby spinach (washed and the stems removed)
¼ cup pine nuts
¼ wedge fresh lemon (the rest could be used for garnishing)
salt and pepper to taste

Using a nonstick skillet, heat 2 tablespoons of olive oil and slide in the salted fish fillets. I use medium to medium-high heat to get a good brown color. Sauté one side of the fish until browned. Flip the fish and cook on the other side until fork tender. (Do not overcook, or fish will be dry.) Drizzle or splash a little fresh lemon juice on top of the fish. Remove fish and place on your warmed serving plates.

Using the same pan, add the other 2 tablespoons of olive oil. Add the shallot and garlic. Sauté until softened (only 1 or 2 minutes). Add the spinach and sauté very quickly until tender crisp (nice green color).

Slide the spinach onto the fish fillets. Sprinkle with pine nuts and serve hot.

If you want an extra garnish, sprinkle chopped fresh tomatoes on top of the spinach. Add a slice of lemon on the side. Goes really well with brown rice.

SANDY BEAUDOIN
Enterprise, OR—KMBI

When everyone is home, they all expect me to make this dish. Our favorite. Quick and easy.

Italian Chicken Artichoke

6 skinless chicken breasts
1 cup mushrooms, cut in half
3 cloves garlic
¼ cup onions
2 cans Italian tomatoes
1 T Italian seasoning
salt and pepper to taste
4 cups cooked rice (I add 3 chicken bouillon cubes to water when making rice.)
1 jar artichokes (can add 2 jars)
1 can black olives

Cut up chicken breasts or leave whole. Cook chicken on stove until done. Sauté mushroom, garlic, and onions. Put all ingredients except artichoke and olives in baking dish, and cook for 30 minutes at 375°. In the last 5 minutes add black olives and artichoke to main dish, and finish baking. Serve over rice.

NOELLE BOYSEN-LEDBETTER
Rock Island, IL—WLUJ

This recipe has been used for two generations and never altered. It's easy, very inexpensive, and, most of all, most kids love it.

Shelby Rae's Chili

1½ pounds ground beef
2 small cans tomato paste
2 cans tomato soup
1 small onion
1 large can Brooks beans
2 T chili powder
3 cups water
¼ stick margarine

Brown ground beef with butter and chopped onion. Drain. Using a 4-quart Dutch oven, add tomato paste and soup, and stir. Add beans and chili powder, and mix well. Mix in water. Cover and cook on low heat for one hour, stirring occasionally; then simmer for half hour.

Hint: Throw it in a Crock-Pot all together; mix well. Cook on high 3 hours or 6 hours on low. It turns out the same and takes just 5 minutes to put together.

Karin Brown
Eau Claire, WI—WHEM

This recipe is one of my favorites from my mom. I like to serve it for company because it looks like a lot of work, but it really isn't that difficult! With all the wonderful alfredo sauces available in a jar now, it's easy to make fettuccini Alfredo as a quick side dish to go along with it.

Chicken Breasts in Sour Cream

6–8 skinless, boneless chicken breasts
2 cups sour cream
¼ cup lemon juice
2 tsp. salt

4 tsp. Worcestershire sauce
1 T garlic powder (can use more)
½ tsp. paprika
½ tsp. pepper
bread crumbs (in shaker can)
2 sticks butter

Wash the chicken and pat dry. In a large bowl combine the sour cream, lemon juice, salt, Worcestershire sauce, garlic powder, paprika, and pepper. Put chicken into this mixture, coating each piece. Cover and refrigerate all day or overnight.

Preheat oven to 350°. Remove chicken from sauce and roll in bread crumbs to coat well. Roll up chicken pieces and place in a baking dish, seam-side down. Melt the butter and pour half over the chicken. Bake at 350° for 45 minutes. Pour the remaining butter over the chicken and bake for another 15 minutes.

Chicken may be frozen after it is breaded. Wrap in individual packages for added convenience. Remove chicken from freezer the morning of the day to be baked. Leftovers are a delicious cold snack!

Tina M. Chaney
Sneads Ferry, NC—WLPG

I found this recipe on the side of a penne noodle box. My youngest son fell in love with this recipe and has since called it Poor Man's Lasagna. He made this recipe for his youth group's ministry meal last year. This recipe is very kid-friendly.

Mastasella Casserole

Yield: 12–15 servings

1 16 oz. box penne noodles (cooked)
2 26 oz. cans Del Monte spaghetti sauce (any flavor; I use traditional)
1 lb. package Hillshire Farms smoked sausage or kielbasa (pre-cooked, cut in bite-sized pieces)
4 cups mozzarella cheese, shredded

Mix the cooked noodles (cooled), spaghetti sauce, sausage, and 2 cups of mozzarella cheese, and place in a 9x14" baking pan. Cook at 350° for about 25 minutes. Remove from oven and sprinkle the remaining 2 cups of mozzarella cheese on top. Place back in oven for another 5–10 minutes or until cheese is melted.

Let cool for 10–15 minutes, then slice and serve with your favorite salad and French bread. This recipe can be halved . . . or divide it into two containers, and freeze one for another time. Just leave the cheese off the top until after it has baked.

Linda Churchill
Barrington, IL—WMBI

I am a registered dietitian, so I try to find healthy yet delicious recipes. Everyone seems to love this dish.

Winter White Ravioli

4 servings

1 9 oz. package fresh 4-cheese ravioli
1 15–16 oz. can great northern or navy beans, rinsed and drained
1 (14½ oz.) can diced tomatoes, undrained
½ tsp. dried basil
½ tsp. dried oregano
⅛ tsp. crushed red pepper
6 cups chopped fresh escarole or spinach
¼ cup water
¼ cup (1 oz.) grated Asiago cheese

Cook pasta according to package directions, omitting salt and fat. Combine the beans, tomatoes, basil, oregano, and red pepper in a large saucepan. Bring to a boil, and stir in spinach. Cover, reduce heat, and simmer 3 minutes or until spinach is wilted. Stir in pasta and ¼ cup water; cook 1 minute or until thoroughly heated. Sprinkle with cheese.

I double or triple this recipe—very easy!

CHERYL DUNLOP
Nashville, TN

Greetings from the editor of this cookbook! (No, I didn't try every recipe.) When I lived in Chicago, I heard Midday Connection on WMBI (and once I was even a last-minute substitute guest, interviewed about my first book, *Follow Me as I Follow Christ*), but these days I'm out of MBN range.

My parents, Herb and Jean Dunlop—both now deceased—met and married in Nigeria, and my oldest brother, Paul, was born there. They had seven children; I'm number five. They picked this recipe up in Nigeria from British missionaries, though it probably has roots in India. It has been modified extensively through the years by various members of my family, so it's truly an international dish.

This is a favorite meal of nearly everyone in my family. I serve it buffet-style, and it's my favorite guest meal. When guests try it for the first time, they usually take only a few toppings (and adults avoid the marshmallows). Almost invariably they go back for generous seconds (taking marshmallows the second time), and men often take thirds.

The standing joke in my family, after everyone has stuffed themselves on curry, is "What's for dessert?" Obviously, this meal is too filling (and has too many sweet things included) for anyone to need dessert.

All quantities are approximate, since this is served buffet-style. I keep back surplus of every topping and refill serving dishes when everyone has gone through the line once, knowing that seconds and thirds will be desired.

Pile-It-High Curry

Yield: about 6 servings

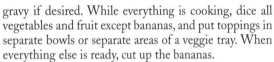

at least 6 cups cooked rice
1½ lbs. chicken, cut up (can also use lamb, my mom's original meat; I've never had it)
½ lb. sausage, cut up
vegetable oil
curry powder to taste (Spice Islands brand is not spicy, but mild and a bit sweet)

Toppings

1 large tomato, diced
½ onion, diced
1–2 cups shredded coconut
1 cup miniature marshmallows (more if many children are present)
2 cups peanuts and/or cashews
1–2 cups blueberries, mandarin oranges, or diced pineapple
2–3 bananas, diced (wait till the last minute, or dip in lemon juice)
curry powder so guests can add more

Cook sausage and set aside. Cut up chicken. Prepare oil for sautéeing chicken by adding curry powder and then heating it (or boil the chicken with curry in the water). Set rice on to cook (optional: add 1–2 tsp. curry powder to the water). Sauté or boil chicken, drain, and then mix sausage and chicken together. Prepare a light

gravy if desired. While everything is cooking, dice all vegetables and fruit except bananas, and put toppings in separate bowls or separate areas of a veggie tray. When everything else is ready, cut up the bananas.

Curry is served rice first, then the meat (with gravy over it if desired—I don't make a gravy), then any and all toppings that people wish to add. It doesn't look like the flavors will go together, but they do—and this is also a very colorful meal.

TAMMY DURST

Bradenton, FL—WKES

This is warm and good, and it must be healthy because it has spinach in it. We have had many pans of it at a huge family Christmas dinner.

I have made it for company and taken it to a family with a new baby.

Turkey and Cheese Lasagna Bake

Yield: 8 servings

2 (10¼ oz.) cans cream of chicken soup (or cream of mushroom)
½ cup milk
⅓ cup chopped onion
½ tsp. chicken bouillon
1 tsp. pepper
1 tsp. salt
½ cup sour cream
1 (15 oz.) container ricotta cheese
1 egg, beaten
½ lb. lasagna noodles, cooked and drained
3 cups chopped cooked turkey or chicken
2 (10 oz.) pkg. frozen chopped spinach, thawed and drained
2 cups shredded American cheese
2 cups shredded mozzarella cheese

Cook cream of chicken soup, milk, onion, bouillon, pepper, and ½ tsp salt in a medium saucepan until heated. Stir constantly. Blend sour cream into above mixture.

In another bowl blend together ricotta cheese, egg, and ½ tsp. salt.

In a 13x9" pan layer ⅓ each of lasagna noodles, chopped turkey, spinach, ricotta mixture, cheeses, and soup mixture. Repeat layers. Cover. Bake at 375° approximately 50 minutes or until hot.

Uncover and bake 10 more minutes. Let stand 5 minutes before cutting.

VICKI FRIZZELL

Dunlap, TN—WMBW

Nacho Cheese Casserole

Easy meal; kids like it.

1 lb. ground beef
1 small package Mahatma yellow rice
1 can Rotel tomatoes and green chilies
1 lb. Velveeta
milk—enough to melt Velveeta
nacho cheese Doritos

Brown beef and drain. Cook rice according to directions on package. Add a little milk to Velveeta and melt. Add Rotel to Velveeta. Mix beef, rice, and cheese. Pour into a casserole dish and bake at 350° until casserole bubbles. Remove casserole from oven, top with crushed Doritos, and return to oven for 5 minutes.

Kristen Hamilton
Meadville, PA—WVME

I'm a stay-at-home-mom to a two-year-old and a ten-month-old. I don't get a lot of time to cook, and this dish is very simple, quick, and inexpensive. Everyone likes it and it's very diverse—many ingredients can be substituted to create slightly different meals. It can also be created on the stovetop or in the oven.

Bow Tie Pasta with Chicken and Peas

8 oz. pasta (bow tie pasta or elbow macaroni)
2 cups coarsely chopped, cooked chicken or
** 10 oz. prepackaged, precooked diced chicken**
8–10 oz. frozen peas (cooked)
10½ oz. can cream of chicken soup
½ cup low-fat milk
Optional: ½ tsp. dried rosemary or thyme
⅛ tsp. pepper
½ cup grated Parmesan cheese

To bake: Heat oven to 425°. Cook pasta in Dutch oven or large pot. Drain. Return pasta to pot. Add all ingredients except Parmesan. Mix thoroughly. Sprinkle with parmesan. Bake 10 minutes.

To make on stovetop: Cook pasta. Drain. Cook peas. Drain. Combine all ingredients except Parmesan in saucepan. Mix thoroughly and heat through. Sprinkle with Parmesan before serving.

Beef variation: Substitute 1 lb. browned, drained ground beef for chicken. Substitute cream of mushroom soup for cream of chicken soup. With this variation, we like to use carrots instead of peas.

Tuna variation: Substitute one can of tuna fish (small or large depending on how much meat you want) for chicken. Substitute cream of celery soup for cream of chicken soup. Either peas or carrots work well with this variation.

JoAnne Hidalgo
Land O' Lakes, FL—WKES

My grandma Whitnah and her sister Helen were the best of friends. In fact, they fondly referred to each other as "friend." They were always an inspiration to me, and I know there was a celebration in heaven when they went up to be with Jesus at their appointed times. They especially were a pinnacle of what being a Christian is—in every sense of the word. Each loved Jesus with all her heart, soul, and mind, in addition to loving her neighbor, as the Bible instructs (Matt. 22:37–39). Their godly impression on me was a fond and enduring reflection of what footsteps I hoped to emulate one day.

Whenever there was someone (in their church, the neighborhood, a friend, etc.) who needed a meal, they whipped up something. Christmas and Easter were spent at their house with friends and family. I especially remember one occasion when they made a meal that included a yummy chicken casserole.

When I was older, I asked for the recipe. My husband marks it as "one of his favorites," and I have been fortunate to carry on the tradition of making that meal for others. I have been blessed to be able to provide this meal many times through the "Meals Ministry" program at my church.

I have received many rave reviews for Grandma and Aunt Helen's Chicken Casserole. It's easy to make and quite affordable . . . and yummy!

Chicken Casserole

Yield: 6 servings

1 whole chicken (approx 3½–4 lbs.), skinned
1 tsp. salt
1 tsp. pepper
2 cans (10½ oz. each) cream of chicken soup
½ cup mayonnaise
2 stalks celery, chopped
¼ cup onion if desired (chopped)
1 can (8 oz.) water chestnuts (diced)
grated cheddar cheese (approx. 12 to 16 oz.)
crushed potato chips

Cook chicken in water to cover until tender (about 1¼ hours) with salt and pepper. Cool, bone, and chop. Mix soup and mayonnaise. Add celery, onion, and water chestnuts. Put all in a greased 2-quart casserole dish. Sprinkle generously with cheese. Before baking, sprinkle top with crushed potato chips. Bake at 425° for 25 to 30 minutes. Cool and serve.

JULIA JAST
Homer Glen, IL—WMBI

As a busy mom of eleven, I rely on this recipe to satisfy my hungry crew. Served with corn bread muffins, it is an easy meal all in one pan.

Beef Stew for a Crew

1½ lbs. ground beef
11 oz. can cream of mushroom soup
3 potatoes, diced
6 onions, chopped
1 bunch celery (6 stalks), sliced
1 lb. baby carrots
16 oz. bag frozen corn or peas
salt and pepper to taste

Crumble raw meat in the bottom of a small, covered roasting pan and spread soup over the top. Layer ingredients in the order given over the meat and soup. Add salt and pepper to taste. Bake at 400° for 1 hour.

SANDY JOHNSON
Naperville, IL—WMBI

This is an easy, inexpensive recipe and both my husband and my twenty-one-year-old son really like it. The sauce has a little bit of a kick to it, but it's not too spicy or hot, and the leftovers (if there are any) are tasty as well.

Cheesy Beef-Filled Corn Bread Squares

6 servings

1 lb. lean ground beef
¾–1 cup chopped onion
1 clove garlic, minced (or 1 tsp. prepared minced garlic)
½ cup ketchup
1 pkg. corn bread mix (such as Jiffy)
1 egg
⅓ cup milk
1½ cups shredded cheddar cheese or shredded Mexican cheese blend, divided
1 can stewed tomatoes or diced tomatoes with garlic
1 T Worcestershire sauce
2 T chopped green chilies
2 T chopped green pepper
cornstarch

Brown ground beef, onions, and garlic in nonstick skillet. Drain fat. Add ketchup and stir to combine.

While beef is browning, prepare corn bread according to package directions. Stir into corn bread mixture half of the shredded cheese. In a greased 8" square baking dish, spread half of the corn bread mixture. Then spread the ground beef mixture on top of that, and sprinkle the remaining cup of cheese over the ground beef. Spoon the remaining corn bread mixture over the top of the cheese and spread evenly to the sides of the dish. Bake in a 350° oven for 25 minutes or until corn bread on top is golden brown.

Meanwhile, in a medium saucepan, combine tomatoes, Worcestershire sauce, green chilies, and green pepper. Heat until simmering. Take 2 tablespoons of tomato mixture and combine in a separate bowl with a teaspoon of cornstarch until smooth, and then add to the saucepan. Stir until tomato mixture is thickened. Keep warm until corn bread mixture is finished baking.

To serve, cut 6 squares out of the corn bread mixture and top with the prepared tomato sauce.

CELESTE MALLOY
Cleveland, OH—WCRF

This meal really gets work done at the homes of different family members. Yard work, indoor spring cleaning, and more. It takes about two hours to make. Everybody loves this, kids and adults, but it is not for someone on a diet. The cost is offset by the barter system (getting your house painted).

House-Painting Spaghetti

3 lbs. spaghetti
3 lbs. ground meat (beef or turkey)
seasoning salt
fresh pepper in grinding container
2 lbs. kielbasa, cut in small chunks
3 large green peppers, large diced pieces
2 large onions, diced
4–6 cans Hunts spaghetti sauce
Italian seasoning
¼ cup of sugar
½ cup fresh garlic, diced
1½ lbs. mild cheddar cheese
1½ lbs. sharp cheddar cheese

Have the 20-lb. turkey roaster ready (without the turkey). Cook spaghetti according to package directions for firm noodles. Brown ground meat, adding seasoned salt, 2 turns of ground pepper, and kielbasa. Drain meats well.

Sauté green peppers, onions, and garlic.

Simmer 4 cans of spaghetti sauce on low heat in a large pot, and add sautéed veggies, Italian seasoning, sugar. Mix sauce, meat, and spaghetti (in very large pot). If the sauce is not thick, simmer additional cans of sauce with 1 tablespoon of sugar and seasoning salt.

In the large roaster, layer the spaghetti and the cheeses. Bake for 1 hour at 350°. Serve with salad and warm bread. Call everyone you know with a paintbrush.

JAN MARLOWE
Fort Myers Beach, FL—WSOR

My sons loved these linguica sloppy joes as a Saturday noon meal.

Linguica Sloppy Joes

1 lb. Portuguese linguica, crumbled
1 lb. lean ground beef
1 chopped green pepper
1 large can tomato sauce
a few drops of hot sauce, if desired
4 bulkie rolls

Sauté green pepper in oil. Add crumbled linguica and beef, and cook until meat is brown. Add tomato sauce and heat through. Add hot sauce, if desired. Serve in a bulkie roll.

NINI MASSEY
Land O' Lakes, FL—WKES

Easy and delicious for all the kids; my husband also loves and can make it, even though he doesn't usually like Italian/pasta sauce that much. Quick and inexpensive.

3-Cheese Chicken Parmesan

4 chicken breasts
3 beaten raw eggs
Italian breading (Vigo Bread Crumbs
    recommended)
Romano & Parmesan cheeses
olive oil
1 jar spaghetti sauce (recommended: fire-roasted
    garlic tomato by Classico)
Optional: 1 piece of fresh leaf Italian basil
approx. 8 oz. soft mozzarella cheese

Each breast should be flattened out using a roller or simply cut long ways into 4 pieces per breast, then flattened. Dip uncooked chicken in beaten raw egg, and dust with your favorite Italian breading. Add Romano and Parmesan cheeses to breading if not already included.

On stovetop, sear both sides of each lightly breaded chicken breast at medium temperatures in olive oil, 1 minute per side till golden brown.

While searing, prepare pan for baking. Empty 1 jar of spaghetti sauce in baking pan. Preheat oven to 375°.

Remove seared chicken from pan and place to swim in sauce, but note, not submerged entirely by sauce! Cover each piece of chicken by adding one piece of fresh leaf Italian basil (optional); then cover with soft mozzarella cheese (not optional)—which is sliced to your desired thickness and placed on top of each seared chicken breast in pan. Note: The mozzarella should not turn brown baking. Bake at 375° for 20–25 minutes; do not overcook.

Serve hot with warmed sauce-less pasta noodles of choice, buttered preferable.

Additional side, my favorite: Serve with sliced veggies such as zucchini and/or squash, lightly pan sautéed in olive oil (while chicken is in oven), 1 to 2 minutes per side, with pinch of sea salt and white or black pepper along with a light dash of Italian seasoning.

KIM MORRISON
McCordsville, IN—WGNR

My husband is the cook in our family and I have become spoiled. I am the "cleaner upper" and cook only occasionally. However, of the handful of recipes I do prepare, my family loves this one. Easy and healthy too.

Cantonese Chicken

3 boneless, skinless chicken breasts
3 T water
3 T soy sauce (may use light soy sauce)
1 packet dry spaghetti sauce
1 small can water chestnuts, drained
1 small can mushrooms, drained
1 15 oz. can diced tomatoes
1 medium green pepper, slivered

Cut chicken into bite-sized pieces. Mix water, soy sauce, and spaghetti sauce together. Marinate chicken in mixture in the refrigerator for a half hour. In a medium bowl, add water chestnuts, mushrooms, tomatoes with juice, and slivered green pepper. In a skillet, stir-fry chicken in the oil on medium-high until done—5 to 7 minutes. Turn heat back to medium. Add vegetable mixture to the skillet and heat through. Serve over brown rice.

MICHELE ODSTRCILEK
Lemont, IL—WMBI

I get home from work at 5:15 p.m., and on Wednesday nights I'm at Awana by 6:30. On Sundays I have choir practice at 5 p.m., so this recipe is a great helper on either of these busy days! It's inexpensive also. And this is great in the summer when it's too hot to go outside and grill and too hot inside to cook over the stove. My family really likes these !

Amazing Beef

Yield: 4-6 servings

4–5 lb. bottom round roast
3–5 garlic cloves, sliced in half
32 oz. jar of Peppercini peppers (hot or mild)
optional: 1–2 T beef base
French bread or any sub-type rolls
optional: 1 small jar of horseradish to spread on
    the bread

Cut slits in roast and insert a piece of garlic in each slit. Put roast in Crock-Pot and pour the entire jar of Peppercinis, juice and all, over beef, and add beef base (optional). Cook on low 8–10 hours till meat falls apart. Then take 2 forks and shred the meat. Put on bread of your choice, spread with horseradish, and enjoy! There will be enough juice in the Crock-Pot to add a little to your bread also. Serve with soup or a salad.

DEBI OWINYO
Bonners Ferry, ID—KMBI

This recipe was given to me by my sister in Canada (although I increased the salsa from ¼ cup). It is special because it is an easy and quick way to make enchiladas, which my family loves. I would say it is both quick and kid-friendly (with supervision).

Zesty Chicken Tortilla Bake

⅔ cup Miracle Whip
¼ cup flour
2 cups milk
2 cups grated cheddar cheese, divided
3 cups diced, cooked chicken or turkey
⅓ cup salsa
¼ cup chopped parsley (or 2 T dried parsley)
12 flour tortillas (6")

In medium saucepan blend Miracle Whip (or mayo with scant tablespoon honey) and flour. Whisk in milk. Cook and stir over medium heat until sauce comes to a boil and thickens. Stir in 1½ cup cheese. Reserve 1 cup sauce. Stir chicken, salsa, and parsley into remaining sauce.

Prepare 13x9" baking dish by pouring a thin layer of chicken broth over bottom.

Spoon ⅓ cup of this mixture onto each tortilla. Wrap tortilla around filling. Place filled tortillas seam side up, in two rows, in baking dish. Spoon reserved sauce across centers of filled tortillas. Top with remaining cheese. Bake at 375° for 25 minutes.

CLARISSA PARIZEAU
Conway, SC—WLPG

I wanted to make something special one day for my husband when he came home from being away in the military (he served 22 years). My children wanted to help. So we came up with our version of chicken cordon bleu.

Chicken Parizeau

thawed chicken breast halves, skinless
cheese (low-fat if trying to be healthy)
sliced meat (luncheon meat or leftovers)
parsley
oregano
poultry seasoning

Preheat oven to 350°. Wash the chicken thoroughly. Lay on paper plate smooth side down. Layer your choice of meats and cheese. Sprinkle with seasonings. Roll the chicken, using toothpicks where needed to hold closed. Spray pan with nonstick spray. Place chicken in pan. Cook 30 minutes. Turn over, and cook until done.

VICKI POTTER
Springfield, IL—WLUJ

This was the first Asian home-cooked dinner my children learned to enjoy, and it stretches one round steak to feed six people. Kid-friendly and inexpensive.

Chinese Pepper Steak

Yield: 6 servings

3 cups hot cooked rice prepared as package
    recommends
1 lb. lean round steak
1 T paprika
2 cloves garlic, crushed (or 2 T garlic from a jar,
    garlic flakes, or 1 T garlic powder)
2 T canola oil or butter
1½ cups beef broth (2 bouillon cubes dissolved
    in 1½ cups of water)
1 cup sliced green onions
2 green peppers, cut in strips
2 T cornstarch
¼ cup water
¼ cup soy sauce
2 large fresh tomatoes, cut into eighths

While rice is cooking, pound steak to ¼-inch thickness. Cut into ¼-inch wide strips. Sprinkle meat with paprika and garlic, and allow to stand while preparing other ingredients. Using a large skillet, brown meat in oil. Add beef broth. Cover and simmer 30 minutes. Stir in onions and green peppers. Cover and cook 5 minutes more. Blend cornstarch, water, and soy sauce into meat mixture. Cook, stirring until clear and thickened—about 2 minutes. Add tomatoes and stir gently. Serve over beds of hot fluffy rice.

MAUREEN PRANGHOFER
Golden Valley, MN—KTIS

I've been married to my wonderful husband, Paul, for almost thirty years. His favorite food is corned beef hash. In this recipe I found an easy way to make it, getting cooked corned beef from the deli, and we both love it.

Corned Beef Hash

Yield: 4 servings

3 cups cooked boiled potatoes, cubed
2 cups cooked chopped
    corned beef, cubed
½ cup finely chopped onion
about ½ cup milk
½ tsp. salt
dash of pepper
3–4 T butter or margarine

Combine potatoes, corned beef, and onions; add enough of the milk to moisten, and the salt and pepper. Melt butter in a skillet. Spread beef mixture evenly in pan and cook over low heat about 20 minutes or until well browned on bottom. Turn in sections with spatula and brown other side. Or fold over as for omelet, if desired. Note: The milk used in corned beef hash and roast beef hash is what makes the hash get nice and golden and crispy.

PURI PURTA
Grafton, OH—WCRF

I was able to adapt this recipe to be gluten free (no wheat) without changing the taste. Everyone to whom I have served it raves about it. They don't know it doesn't contain wheat. My son, who doesn't like spinach, loves it. It is quick and easy to make. Can be prepared and refrigerated the day before it is baked.

Crustless Spinach Quiche

Yield: 6–8 servings

10 oz. package frozen spinach, thawed,
    drained, chopped
3 eggs
12 oz. cottage cheese
3 T Buckwheat flour (can use white flour if not
    wheat sensitive)
2 T butter, melted
8 oz. shredded cheddar cheese

Preheat oven to 350°. Mix all ingredients together. Pour into a greased deep-dish pie pan or 9x9" pan. Bake for approximately 1 hour, or until edges are brown and toothpick is clean.

 **JENNY QUAAS**
Roseburg, OR—KGRV

Our church has an annual chili cook-off at our Harvest Celebration. Last October this recipe tied for first place! It's quick and easy and uses everyday ingredients. My friends from Texas refuse to call it chili, so you may want to call it Scarecrow Chowder. It's easy to fix and does great in a Crock-Pot. It's heart-healthy and quick.

Scarecrow Chili

whole roasted chicken
4 15 oz. cans great northern beans, rinsed and drained
1 14 oz. can diced stewed tomatoes
1 4 oz. can diced green chilies
1 14 oz. can chicken broth (save can)
2 14 oz. cans water

1 fresh jalapeño pepper, chopped
1 rib of celery, chopped
½ white onion, chopped
1 garlic clove, chopped
1 T chili powder
½ T ground cumin

To save time, buy the chicken precooked. Cut chicken into bite-sized pieces. Mix all ingredients in a large pot. I use a Crock-Pot and cook on low for 4–6 hours. The longer it cooks, the better the flavor is. Add garlic salt and fresh cilantro to taste. Garnish with a slice of avocado and a squeeze of lime juice. Top with tortilla chips if desired.

DANETTE REEVES
Calhoun, TN—WMBW

Kids can help stir ingredients and wrap sandwiches. This is a good hot sandwich that we have used for fun times in our family. We sometimes have it on the night we decorate the Christmas tree, along with other special goodies. Sometimes we have it at a time when we can play a family game, or we take it along when we have a bonfire. Goes great with chips and salsa. It is an easy fix and sets the scene for a fun, intimate evening with an opportunity for great conversation.

Hot Corned Beef Sandwiches

12 oz. can corned beef
¼ cup chili sauce
¼ cup chopped onions
2 eggs, hard-boiled and diced
3 T mayonnaise
2 heaping cups shredded cheddar cheese
12 hot dog buns (whole wheat or white)

Preheat oven to 350º. Mash corned beef until no large lumps remain. Mix in all other ingredients, except cheese and buns, until smooth. Add cheddar cheese and stir well. Spoon evenly into the 12 hot dog buns. Wrap buns individually in aluminum foil. Place on cookie sheet and bake for 20 minutes.

DIANE ROE
New London, WI—WRVM

This is my husband's favorite food, and he makes it once a month. And when he makes it, I get to help him make it, and when I get to cook with him it's like a romance that starts in the kitchen. It's good quality time to reconnect with each other. I think this is on the healthy side of the menu.

White Chili

Yield: 16–24 servings

3 lbs. boneless, skinless chicken
3 large onions, chopped
3 garlic cloves (pressed)
1 lb. sliced fresh mushrooms
4 15 oz. cans cannellini beans (don't drain the beans)
4 15 oz. cans northern beans
3 tsp. cumin
3 tsp. cilantro
3 tsp. white pepper
1 tsp. cayenne pepper

Boil chicken breast until cooked through, and cut into bite-sized chunks. Sauté onions and garlic until tender. In a big pot, place chicken, onions, garlic, mushrooms, beans, and the spices. Simmer until heated through and serve. To make it thinner add water. I have also put it in a slow cooker and simmered on low all day until I want to eat it.

DORIS SEWELL
Trussville, AL—WLJR

*This recipe is the **only** thing that I can guarantee my entire family will love and eat every time. I am a working mom, and I can cook the ingredients requiring precooking at night, assemble everything in the slow cooker, and it is ready to top the pasta the next night when I get home. The best part is that my family wants it again the next night! And it tastes better with time. It is definitely a crowd pleaser.*

Best Ever Spaghetti Sauce

2 T extra-virgin olive oil
1 medium onion, chopped
1 green pepper, chopped
2 cloves garlic, minced
1 pkg. fresh sliced mushrooms
2 lbs. ground chuck/beef
1 lb. ground sausage
2 small cans tomato paste
2 jars your favorite spaghetti sauce
spices (salt, pepper, garlic powder, basil,
    oregano, bay leaf)
several good dashes Louisiana hot sauce
lots of Worcestershire sauce
    (approximately ⅛ cup)

Heat pan to medium heat with olive oil. Add onion and green pepper and sauté until translucent. Add beef and sausage; break up into smaller pieces and brown until cooked through. Drain mixture and put it into a slow cooker. Add the tomato paste and mix thoroughly with the meat combination. Pour in the jars of spaghetti sauce, garlic, and mushrooms, and mix thoroughly. Add spices in generous portions (the spicier the better) and the hot sauce and Worcestershire sauce. Let the sauce cook all day on low in the slow cooker.

RALYN SNYDER
Springfield, OH—WEEC

This is a recipe that my husband's family has passed on to me. It is a favorite every place I have taken it, and it is easy to throw in a slow cooker and have it ready to feed your family after a hard day of work.

Chicken Kelly

boneless chicken breasts (or tenders)
several eggs, beaten
garlic salt
Italian bread crumbs
mushrooms
diced onions
chicken broth
Monterey Jack cheese, sliced (or Muenster or Swiss)

Exact amounts of ingredients should be adjusted accordint to how many people you are serving. Cut chicken breasts into smaller, bite-sized pieces and tenderize. Mix together eggs and garlic salt, and marinate chicken at least overnight (24 hours is suggested, but not required). Drain off liquid and dredge in bread crumbs. Brown chicken on both sides in a skillet briefly—I use olive oil. Sauté mushrooms and onions in the same skillet. Place breaded breasts in an oven dish and cover with chicken broth (or water). Top with mushrooms, onions, and sliced cheese. Bake for 1 hour at 350°. This can also be placed in a Crock-Pot to serve at your next potluck.

SALLY SOMSEL
Traverse City, MI—WLJN

When my mother got married she declared that she couldn't cook. But she learned alongside my grandmother on my father's side. My mother was a great student and eventually a great cook. She collected all sorts of recipes. Every once in a while, it wouldn't be a good one. My father never complained, but I do remember him saying, "You can lose that recipe." Even though she has left this earthly life for heaven, the recipes she left behind remind us all of her love of family and of cooking. Even her grandchildren, who are now in their early 40s, love Grandma's Baked Fried Chicken and her wonderful rolls that we serve at large family gatherings.

This chicken is kid-friendly with adult supervision; it can be made healthier by removing the chicken skin, and is quick to make (less than 1 hour) and inexpensive. Preparation time if using cut-up chicken is 10 minutes; then put it into the oven for 55 minutes, and use that time to prepare the other items for your dinner.

Simple and Delicious Oven-Fried Chicken

Yield: 4–5 servings

1 large cut-up chicken (remove the skin if you wish)
⅓ cup vegetable oil
⅓–½ cup butter
1 cup all-purpose flour
1 tsp. salt
1 tsp. garlic salt
2 tsp. black pepper
2¼ tsp. paprika

Put oil and butter in a shallow roasting pan, place in oven at 375° to melt butter, and then set aside. In a large paper lunch sack, combine the dry ingredients and shake to mix.

Roll the chicken pieces one at a time in the melted butter and oil, then drop into the sack and shake to fully coat chicken pieces with the flour mixture. Place on a plate until all pieces are coated. Leave any excess butter and oil in pan.

Place chicken in the pan skin side down. Bake at 375° for 45 minutes. Remove from oven; turn chicken pieces over and bake 10 minutes longer or until crust begins to bubble.

DORETTA SPEICHER
Manns Choice, PA—WTLR

My aunt brought this hearty stew over after our second baby was born. We enjoyed it so much I had to have the recipe. Because it is so simple yet so satisfying, I prepare this dish often: for our family, for guests, or even for delivering it to other new moms. I often use a chuck roast instead of stewing meat, which gives it even richer flavor. And just like my aunt did a couple of years ago, I serve this stew with fresh bread and a crisp salad.

Essie's Busy Day Stew

1¼ lb. beef stewing meat (or 2 lb. chuck roast)
4 potatoes
2 carrots
2 cups diced turnips/potatoes
2 cups diced celery
1 cup chopped onion
1 pkg. onion soup mix
1 tsp. celery seed
1 14 oz. can tomatoes
1 cup water
salt and pepper
2–4 T minute tapioca
2 T sugar

Cut stewing meat into small pieces. Dice potatoes and carrots. Put all ingredients together in roaster. Bake at 250° for 5–6 hours. Delicious and tender.

CAROLINE STINE
Chambersburg, PA—WCRH

This recipe is special to me, because it is a change from the usual. I would say this recipe is inexpensive and rather quick; once the chicken is cooked, it's just a matter of putting it together.

Tasty Mexican Chicken

1 can cream of chicken soup
13 oz. bag crushed Doritos (nacho flavor—use about ½ to ¾ of the bag)
16 oz. jar of salsa
2–2½ cups of cooked chicken
1–1½ cups of grated cheese

Mix together the chicken, soup, and salsa. In an 11x7" glass dish, layer the crushed Doritos, then the chicken mixture, then the cheese. Bake at 350° till the cheese is melted and it bubbles together (about 20–30 minutes). Let set before serving.

CHERI TEW
Lakeland, FL—WKES

My mom usually didn't cook this dish unless company was coming over, and many times she served it by request. Today when I smell this dish cooking, I am reminded of warm times of fellowship with friends and family. Unfortunately, many kids today do not know about homemade enchiladas; they only know about Taco Bell. Believe me, they are missing out! Kid-friendly, if they like Mexican food.

Hamburger Enchiladas

Yield: 8 servings

2 T cooking oil
1¼ lb. hamburger
1 cup chopped onion, divided
2 6 oz. cans tomato paste
1 12 oz. can mixed vegetable juice (V-8)
1 cup water
2 tsp. chili powder
1 tsp. red pepper
1 tsp. garlic salt
1 tsp. salt
¼ tsp. black pepper
½ lb. grated cheddar cheese
24 corn tortillas

In cooking oil, brown hamburger and ½ cup chopped onion. Add the rest of the ingredients, except for the rest of the onions, the cheese, and the tortillas, and simmer 45 minutes. Dip each tortilla in hot oil just long enough to soften it. Drain on a paper towel, and spread 2 tablespoons meat sauce on each tortilla. Sprinkle with grated cheddar cheese and chopped onion. Roll up and place in shallow baking dish. Sprinkle tops with remaining cheddar cheese and onions. Pour 1 cup meat sauce over all. Bake at 350° for 15 minutes. Serve with additional sauce.

LYNNE THRASHER
Roanoke, VA—Online listener

This is a dish that my family is crazy about. It is probably not healthy, but once in a while we just have to have it.

Thrasher Family Poppy Seed Chicken

2 cups cooked and diced chicken
1 can cream of chicken soup
8 oz. sour cream
2 T ground poppy seeds
1 sleeve Ritz-type crackers, crumbled
1 stick melted butter

Combine first 4 ingredients in a casserole dish. Top with buttered crackers. Bake at 350° for about 25 minutes.

MARY VOVES, JANE VANHELDEN, SANDRA THON, AND RON GOVIN
Holmen and Eau Claire, WI—WHEM

This was a family favorite of ours. It's in memory of our parents, Walter and Beatrice Govin, who were both beautiful people inside and out. They were loving and caring people, and they will remain in our hearts forever.

Saucy Meat Loaves

Makes 6

1½ lbs. ground beef
¾ cup oats
1½ tsp. salt
¼ tsp. pepper
¼ cup onion
1 egg (beaten)
¾ cup milk

Topping

⅓ cup catsup
1 T firmly packed brown sugar
1 T mustard

Combine all ingredients thoroughly. Shape into 6 individual loaves in shallow baking pan. Combine all ingredients of topping, and spread over top. Bake at 350° for 35 to 40 minutes.

THOMAS WHEELER
West Palm Beach, FL—WRMB

This was the first dish I concocted after becoming a Christian eight years ago. It isn't too expensive and not hard to make. You can also vary the "heat" to suit your family. It's the best chili I've ever eaten!

Tom's Roasted Pepper Chili

2 lbs. ground beef
3 cans pinto beans *or*
   2 cans pinto and
   1 can chili beans
   (15 oz. cans)
2 medium onions
3 serranos
3 jalapeños
1 poblano or green pepper
olive oil
½ cup strong beef broth
½–¾ 6 oz. can tomato paste
1 heaping tsp.
   chopped garlic
½ tsp. paprika
¼ tsp. cayenne
   (red) pepper
½ tsp. cilantro
¼ tsp. ginger
¼ tsp. oregano
1 T chili powder
1–2 bay leaves
½ tsp. cumin
¼ tsp. turmeric

Preheat oven to 450°. Dissolve cube of beef broth in ½ cup of hot water and set aside. In an iron skillet, brown ground beef. After oven is hot, place washed vegetables (onions, serranos, jalapeños, and poblano or green pepper) on a rack on a cookie sheet. Roast until underside is blackened; then flip and roast other side until blackened (onion may take longer). Pour off fat from ground beef; absorb most of the fat with a paper towel, but leave meat moist. Add garlic, stir, and heat thoroughly.

After vegetables are blackened, remove to cutting board and coarsely slice. Remove seeds from poblano. Remove all pepper seeds to make a milder chili. Put in a blender and puree.

In a large saucepan, add olive oil and heat on medium-high. Add puree from blender and stir. Stir in beef and garlic mixture. Add tomato paste and beef broth, stirring constantly. In the unwashed blend put 1 can of beans and puree; then add to mixture. Add all other ingredients and stir.

For hotter chili, use 1 lb. of ground beef and 2 cans of beans (1 of them chili beans).

Serve with tortilla chips, shredded cheddar cheese, green onions, and sour cream.

Tip: Put all dry seasonings in a bowl while roasting the vegetables. Throw them into the mix all at once.

JUDY WILLIAMS
Portales, NM—KGLY

Very simple, and easy to make variations to this basic recipe. Even children can make this recipe (mine have—assistance needed with the oven as appropriate). Heart-healthy and good if on a diet.

This recipe can be made ahead and frozen to have on hand in a hurry. We have even used it as a "fund-raiser," and it has been a big hit in the area as well as the state with the Royal Rangers (boys' program) of our churches. My pastor's kids (ages 2–6) are very picky eaters but love this dish. Makes a large dish. I mix and then simmer it in a Crock-Pot.

Taco Stew

2 lb. hamburger
1 chopped onion
1 can chopped green chilies
2 cans tomato sauce
1 large can stewed tomatoes
2 cans pinto beans (do not drain)
1 can yellow hominy (do not drain; corn can be
   substituted for the hominy)
1 can white hominy (do not drain)
1 can Rotel tomatoes
1 package taco seasoning
1 package Hidden Valley Ranch dressing
salt, pepper, garlic to taste

Brown hamburger. Add onion and chilies. Cook until onions are tender. Add rest of ingredients. Serve with grated cheese and tortilla chips, or with corn bread—our favorite.

Side Dishes

ROBIN CHADDOCK
author of Discovering Your Divine Assignment
www.wisdomtreeresources.com

Invitation

*"Look at me. I stand at the door. I knock. If you
hear me call and open the door, I'll come right in
and sit down to supper with you."*
(REVELATION 3:20 THE MESSAGE)

One of my favorite things about my walk with God is that it has seasons. I ponder certain truths and revelations at different seasons. They take hold of my mind and my heart, and I get to play with them for a time—unpacking, observing the reality of the truth in the world and in my life, and spending time chatting with God over what it means and how to tell others.

That's the case in the current season of my walk as I'm being led to ponder the invitations of God through the words of Jesus in the Gospels, then sprinkled through the rest of the New Testament in various, and sometimes surprising, places. God inviting. An invitational God.

Having grown up with a more stern and commanding version of God, this notion of God inviting me is refreshing and delightfully disarming, in some ways.

In Revelation, God invites me to invite Him. My loving, respectful, seeking God asks me to be open and spend time with Him. He doesn't ask that I serve Him the meal. He doesn't ask that I entertain Him during the meal. He doesn't ask that I put on a party for Him and others and wait in the wings. God invites me to invite Him in for a meal . . . together . . . as friends and conversation partners.

That's an invitation I'm inclined to accept.

Corn Pudding

Yield: 6 servings

2 (16 oz.) cans creamed corn
1 (6 oz.) package corn
    muffin mix (we like Jiffy)
2 eggs, beaten
½ cup margarine, melted

Mix all ingredients and pour into a greased 2-quart casserole dish. Bake 45 minutes at 350°. This is a family favorite because it's so easy and the kids themselves can make it. We get requests for repeat performances at all family holidays!

PAUL AND SANDY COUGHLIN
authors of Married But Not Engaged
Sandy's blog: http://reluctantentertainer.blogspot.com
Paul's Web site: http://christianniceguy.com

Dinner Talk–Children Seen *and* Heard

Dinnertime is the most stimulating and important part of our day. After prayer, we go around the table and tell each other what happened during our day. This includes our children's guests. It's their time to share what's on their minds and to answer a few friendly questions if they want. This is how we stay connected. It's lively, a time to let down our hair, and for many of our guests, it's a source of entertainment. There is always lots of laughter and joking.

Some of our young guests aren't used to this amount of banter while eating. A few have been literally speechless at first, but then a desire to be known by others takes hold and they start talking. Some like this new experience so much that they talk until their food gets cold. Being heard makes them feel honored.

The volume of our free-flowing conversations tends to be a few notches higher than what they're used to. And sometimes the conversation isn't exactly "right" or "proper," the way we tend to think of these words in church. But this is the time when we get a chance to point it out without condemning them. They feel comfortable sharing their hearts with us—even when their hearts, like ours on occasion, are in the wrong place. In that way, our dinnertime is also *confession* time.

Dinnertime at the Coughlins is where children are seen *and* heard—even when what they say is exaggerated and negative. We help them handle their feelings instead of saying they shouldn't have any—a fallacy many of us learned as kids.

Like you, we're exhausted at the end of the workday, so sometimes both of us desire to have a much more low-key dinnertime experience. Quiet dinnertimes are far easier, far less time-consuming than robust dinnertimes. But we wouldn't change it for the world.

Dinnertime doesn't feel right unless we've had a good talk, shared our day with others, and had family fellowship. We can't afford *not* to listen to, learn from, and love one another during these special gatherings.

Coughlin Family's Favorite Zucchini Noodles

about 12 zucchini, washed well
olive oil

Take zucchini and create long ribbons with your potato peeler, starting at the top of your zucchini and peeling wide ribbons down the length of it. Continue turning and peeling until you use all of the green, and continue peeling until the zucchini becomes too thin to peel any more. Discard the rest (or use in soup).

Heat a large skillet on medium-high and add olive oil and zucchini "noodles." Sauté for approximately 2–3 minutes. Do not overcook (they will be soggy). Add salt and pepper.

Make your favorite alfredo sauce (or use the recipe below) to add to the noodles, and serve!

Alfredo Sauce

olive oil
about 10 garlic cloves
2 cups whipping cream
1 cup grated Parmesan cheese
salt and pepper to taste

Press garlic cloves and sauté in olive oil in a small fry pan. Add cream and heat on high until it starts to boil; then turn down to low and simmer for 10 minutes. Add cheese, salt, and pepper, and stir until smooth.

SHAUNTI FELDHAHN
author of For Women Only *and* For Men Only
www.shaunti.com

Fellowship Around the Table

I will always associate this simple recipe with good friends and fellowship. Because my husband and I both live far from our families, our church small-group friends have become like a second family. And almost every time we have gathered at someone's home for a potluck dinner and a night of fun and fellowship, this casserole has been on the table.

This sort of fellowship is a lifeline for me: My friends are one of the clearest ways that I can see God expressing His love to me in the day-to-day things of life. When I was twenty-one years old, God first opened my eyes to my need for Jesus through a weekend retreat about "friendship" with Jesus. The theme was that He wasn't just a Master or a King—He also wanted to be our friend. And I had never before understood that God might sometimes use our earthly friends to show us love or to speak into our lives—or to help us know *Him* better.

C. S. Lewis relates that one of the main reasons God wants us in fellowship with other believers is that we get to know Jesus so much better in community, seeing Christ through each other's eyes.

As my travel schedule has gotten more demanding, time with friends around a table has become that much more precious. In the past, my husband and I have often been the ones inviting people over for game nights or dinners, but these days, my friends come looking for me. ("I know you're on a deadline, but you haven't seen anyone in three weeks—put down your work for *one hour* and come to lunch tomorrow!") And in their faithful, pursuing friendship, I see God's love even more.

Broccoli Casserole

Yield: about 6 servings

1 family size package (at least
   20 oz.) frozen, chopped broccoli
8 oz. Velveeta cheese
8 oz. cream cheese
2 T margarine
1 cup milk
1½ sleeves of Ritz crackers

Cook broccoli according to package directions. Put Velveeta in a microwave-safe mixing bowl, and microwave on high 2 minutes. Crush the Ritz crackers; crushing them inside a gallon-size Ziploc bag will reduce mess. (Kids love this task!) Stir the Velveeta and add the cream cheese, margarine, and milk. Microwave on high for another 2 minutes. Stir the cheese sauce well. (You can stir and microwave another 2 minutes if necessary, until the cheese is well blended.)

In a standard casserole dish, create two layers in the following order: broccoli, cheese sauce, Ritz cracker crumbs. Repeat layers. Bake at 350° for 30 minutes.

Note: This recipe is easy to double—just get a bigger dish and double all the ingredients except for the milk, which should only increase to 1½ cups, to avoid making the cheese sauce too liquid. Add more after heating and blending, if needed, to make the cheese mixture a bit creamier.

HOWARD DAYTON
author of Your Money Map
www.crown.org

Sweet Potato Casserole

This is my favorite side dish.

about 4 large sweet potatoes
   (or use canned ones;
   drain well and rinse)
1 can crushed pineapple
   (without sugar, just in
   its own juice)
½ cup raisins
½–1 cup of pecans, crushed
¼ cup real maple syrup, divided
6 apples, peeled and chopped

Cook sweet potatoes, then mash well. Drain some of the liquid from pineapple, and add pineapple to potatoes. Add raisins, pecans, and ⅛ cup maple syrup. Bake at 350° for 30 minutes. Cook apples on stove top with ⅛ cup maple syrup until soft and syrup is cooked down. When sweet potatoes are done, remove from oven and top with cooked apples.

DANNAH GRESH
author of Secret Keeper
www.purefreedom.org

Food and Family

Homemade lasagna, slow-cooked chili, beef potpie, cherry cheesecake, sugar cookies. My mom made the yummiest stuff. I remember her baking this potato-crusted quiche, and none of us could wait for it to be cooled. What memories the table brings to my heart. I delight in creating those same kinds of memories at my table for my teenagers. There's nothing quite as sweet as a night when they are all there and I get to cook, bake, and listen to their life stories. And I am tenacious and stubborn in my insistence that we have as many of them in one week as possible! Can you identify?

Believe it or not, when we do this, we are not just filling up their bellies. Research tells us that we are giving their souls good things as well. (Maybe that's where the term "soul food" came from!) Thirty-three percent of children ages eleven to eighteen eat two or fewer meals with their families each week, reports *American Family Physician*. Researchers found that adolescents who ate more meals with their family suffered significantly lower rates of high-risk activities, were less likely to be depressed, and enjoyed higher grade-point averages.

Deuteronomy 6:7 says, "Impress [God's guidelines for living] on your children. Talk about them when you sit at home and when you walk along the road, when you lie down and when you get up." I can only imagine that most of the "sitting at home" referenced in this verse was done around the table. Let's continue to build a legacy of purity, sobriety, wholeness, and excellence for our children. Pass the pie!

We love this with blueberry streusel muffins in the spring or pumpkin bread in the fall. Great for dainty tea parties with girlfriends or a fabulous easy dinner with your family.

Mom's Potato-Crusted Quiche

3 T vegetable oil
3 cups coarsely shredded potatoes
1 cup grated cheddar cheese
¾ cup deli-shredded ham, chopped
¼ cup chopped onion
1 cup evaporated milk
2 eggs
1 tsp. salt
⅛ tsp. pepper
parsley flakes

In 9" pie pan, stir together vegetable oil and potatoes. Press evenly into a pie crust. Bake at 450° for 15 minutes. Layer cheese, ham, and onion in pie shell. Beat together evaporated milk, eggs, salt, and pepper. Pour liquid over other ingredients. Sprinkle with parsley flakes. Bake at 425° for about 30 minutes or until brown and knife comes out clean. Cool 5 minutes. Cut and serve.

ELLIE KAY
author of Half-Price Living: The Secrets of Living Well on One Income
www.elliekay.com

When I married my husband, he said we could join the military and he would show me the world. What he showed me was 5 babies in 7 years and 15 moves in 20 years! With all those moves and all those babies, we knew that preserving family together time would be critical. One of the ways we've done this is by making the evening meal a priority for the whole family to gather and share challenges as well as chuckles.

A few years back, my mom and dad came through town and joined us for dinner. My mom and I have something in common. I often use my natural Texas accent as a form of self-deprecating humor and my mom, who is Spanish and has a very thick accent, uses hers the same way. The only problem is that others can't always tell the serious attitude from the satirical wit. Philip was 13 at the time and was busily eating his steak while the conversation flowed over and around him. Anyone with teenage boys knows their ability to compartmentalize life into squares, and at the moment, the only thing in my son's "box" was to eat.

My mom sat next to Philip and asked gently, "Eh, Phi-leep, could chew pass de mashed potatoes?" Philip continued to eat as if he didn't hear her.

My mom cleared her throat and spoke a bit louder and somewhat irritated, "Eh, Phi-leep, I, ah, say, could chew pass de mashed potatoes?"

Philip kept eating.

Mom's temper sparked and quickly flamed, "Philip, I say pass de potatoes!" She slapped the back of his head and continued, "What do someone have to do, to get potatoes in dis house?"

Philip's hand went to the back of his head, rubbing the "love pat" my mom had just given him. He looked at me in complete dismay. "Mom?" he asked, as if I were going to intervene and protect him from harm.

I assessed the situation, including my mom's burning eyes and the no-nonsense set of her mouth. I responded in my best Texas drawl, "Son, I'd say that you'd best be passin' those potatoes."

Our kids learn a lot at our dinner table: manners, how to have accomplished conversations, the spiritual applications to life's problems, and how to laugh when you'd rather cry. Some of our dinners are simple. Some are elegant. Some of the conversation is stilted and some of it, every now and then, is profound. It's a time that our children will always remember. And one day, when we are older, if we are so blessed, we'll sit at Philip's table with his children—and ask them to please pass the mashed potatoes.

Killer Mashed Potatoes

Pass the potatoes!

(Pass them on pain of death.)

6 large russet potatoes (peeled and cubed)
½ cup butter
½ cup sour cream
½ cup real cream (or substitute milk)
2 tsp. garlic-pepper-salt
1 cup shredded cheese

Steam or boil potatoes until tender. Place in large mixing bowl, and add butter, sour cream, and slowly add cream until smooth. Mix slowly and add garlic-pepper-salt. Once they are somewhat smooth, increase speed to whip the potatoes and add shredded cheese. Serve at once and with large doses of humor.

Kai Elmer
national music assistant for MBN
(with a little help from my grandmother Evy Elmer)
Kai: Chicago, IL; Evy: Burlington, WA—WMBI

My grandparents immigrated to the U.S. from Denmark after World War II, so no traditional Danish Christmas dinner here in the U.S. is complete without frikadeller. They're so popular, oftentimes, that all the cousins sneak them from the kitchen before they even have a chance to make it to the dinner table!

Frikadeller (Danish Meatballs)

1 lb. ground round beef
½ lb. lean pork
¼ cup flour
1 T cornstarch
2 eggs
1 cup milk
1 onion (grated)
1 tsp. salt
½ tsp. pepper

Grind the meat very fine. Place in mixing bowl and add flour, salt, pepper, and grated onion. Mix well. Add eggs one at a time, continuing to mix. Add milk, and continue mixing. Place desired amount of meat mixture in skillet. Fry in margarine or butter until cooked through.

Chris Segard
Midday Connection engineer

This is one of my favorite side dishes. My wife, Heather, found that this dish is excellent with grilled salmon. A super summer salad for you from the Segard family.

Couscous with Lentils and Spinach

Yield: 6 servings

1 cup chopped onion
2 garlic cloves, minced
2 cups water, divided
½ cup dried lentils
½ cup uncooked couscous
1 T olive oil
10 cups bagged prewashed spinach (about 5 oz.)
    or 5 oz. frozen chopped spinach
1¼ tsp. salt
1 tsp. ground cumin
¼ tsp. freshly ground black pepper

Heat a medium saucepan over medium heat. Coat pan with cooking spray. Add onion to pan; cook 5 minutes or until golden, stirring occasionally. Stir in garlic; cook 30 seconds, stirring constantly. Add 1 cup water and lentils, and bring to a boil. Cover, reduce heat, and simmer 30 minutes or until the lentils are tender.

While lentils cook, bring 1 cup water to a boil in a large saucepan. Gradually stir in couscous and oil. Remove from heat. Add spinach, and cover and let stand 5 minutes. Combine lentil mixture, couscous mixture, salt, cumin, and pepper in a large bowl.

TINA BLACKBURN
Joliet, IL—WMBI

This recipe is special to me because every time I make it, I think of my mom. It was her recipe. It is easy to make and delicious too. It's a huge hit at church potlucks—I always come home with an empty dish!

Mom's Hash Brown Potato Casserole

2 lbs. frozen shredded hash brown potatoes
 (thawed)
¼ tsp. black pepper
2 cups grated cheddar cheese
1 tsp. salt
1 can cream of celery soup
1 cup sour cream
1 medium onion, chopped
2 cups cornflakes, crushed
½ cup melted butter

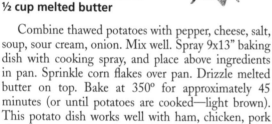

Combine thawed potatoes with pepper, cheese, salt, soup, sour cream, onion. Mix well. Spray 9x13" baking dish with cooking spray, and place above ingredients in pan. Sprinkle corn flakes over pan. Drizzle melted butter on top. Bake at 350° for approximately 45 minutes (or until potatoes are cooked—light brown). This potato dish works well with ham, chicken, pork chops, or sausage.

ANNETTE FORE (ANITA LUSTREA'S MOTHER)
Sarasota, FL—WKZM

This recipe is special because our daughter-in-law gave it to me. She entertains large church groups with great ease. She and our son have raised a godly family. Their daughter is a missionary in Bangladesh and their son is a pilot heading for the mission field soon.

Corn Casserole

Yield: 10–12 servings

1 stick margarine
1 16 oz. can kernel corn, drained
1 16 oz. can creamed corn
8 oz. sour cream
1 8 oz. corn bread mix (such as Jiffy)
 straight from the box

Melt the margarine and add other ingredients. Mix well. Pour into a 9x13" pan. Bake for 1 hour at 325°. This recipe easily doubles; just bake longer.

EVELYN FOX
Princeton, IL—WLUJ

I took this dish to a potluck at the senior center and it became a big hit. This recipe is quick.

Scalloped Pineapple

1 cup margarine, melted
2 cups sugar
3 eggs
1 20 oz. can pineapple tidbits and juice
¼ cup milk
8 slices bread

Melt margarine. Add sugar and eggs; mix well. Add pineapple and milk. Tear bread into small pieces, add to above mixture, and stir well. Pour into 2½-quart casserole dish, lightly sprayed with nonstick spray. Bake at 350° for 1 hour uncovered.

DIANE HARVELL
Springfield, IL—WLUJ

This recipe is special because my mother used to make it regularly. As the youngest of eight, I was always in the kitchen watching. When she had stopped doing a lot of cooking, she asked me to make the coleslaw for a family event. After tasting my coleslaw, she said it tasted even better than what she used to make. This recipe is quick and can be made ahead.

Coleslaw

small head of cabbage
¼ cup chopped onion
¾ cup green pepper
¼ cup red pepper
½ cup sugar
½ cup vinegar
½ tsp. celery seed
½ tsp. mustard seed
½ tsp. salt

Shred cabbage and crisp in ice water. Drain, add onion and peppers, and toss well. Combine sugar and vinegar in saucepan. Heat and stir until sugar is dissolved. When cool, add remaining seasonings. Pour over cabbage. Refrigerate.

Sarah Helms
Winchester, TN—WMBW

I received this recipe about seventeen years ago from a friend, Margaret Green, from my church in Huntsville, AL. She later died of ovarian cancer, and every time I make this recipe I think of her and her love of Jesus Christ. This recipe is a favorite at Thanksgiving and Christmas. I usually double it and make 2 pans because everyone loves it so much. It's also a great recipe to take to covered-dish dinners.

Sweet Potato Casserole

3 medium sweet potatoes, cooked and mashed
⅓ cup milk
¾ cup sugar
1 tsp. vanilla
1 stick butter or margarine, melted
2 eggs

Topping

1 cup brown sugar
⅓ cup melted butter
½ cup flour
1 cup chopped pecans

Peel sweet potatoes, cut into medium to large pieces, and steam until soft enough to mash. Mix all ingredients together and put in 9x13" greased casserole dish. Mix together the topping and sprinkle over sweet potato mixture. Bake at 325° for 30–35 minutes.

Pat Henry
Akron, OH—WCRF

This first recipe came to me from a cousin in PA. I sent it back to PA to my aunt. She gave it to ladies at her church, who put it in a newsletter that went out across the globe—to missionaries and others.

The second recipe was on a cafeteria line in South Carolina. I returned the next year just for the spinach. They didn't have it, but the manager came to my table and offered me a copy of the recipe. I was so excited.

Baked Limas

4 1 lb. cans cooked lima beans, drained
2 medium onions, chopped
1 cup ketchup
2 T mustard
1⅓ cup brown sugar
½ cup syrup
1 lb. bacon: cooked, drained, crumbled
⅛ cup BBQ sauce

Mix all. Place in large casserole dish. Bake 1½ hrs at 350°.

Baked Spinach

1 lb. spinach, chopped (or 1 lb. can drained)
3 oz. vegetable juice
¼ stick margarine
2 oz. saltine crackers, coarsely crushed
2 oz. Spanish onion, chopped
3 oz. cream cheese
½ can cream of celery soup
⅛ tsp. black pepper
3 oz. mild cheddar cheese, shredded

Cook and drain spinach. Mix all except the cheese. Place in 1½–2 quart casserole dish. Top with cheese. Bake 45 minutes at 350°.

Andy and Ann Higgins
Frederick, MD—WCRH

My wife, Ann, and I are avid campers, and every time we get into the woods, one of the first things we crave is our Velvet Vidalia Onions. They can also be made at home in the oven, but then where is the adventure? It actually came to me as an offshoot idea from a long time ago when I was a Boy Scout, when we used to simply squish together some ground beef, sliced potatoes, and onions, wrap it in aluminum foil, and toss it in the campfire. Regardless of the outcome, it was always the perfect dinner for Scouts on a camping trip.

Velvet Vidalia Onions

1 large Vidalia (or other sweet) onion
1 T olive oil
1 T rice wine vinegar
1 T brown sugar
1 T Marsala cooking wine

Peel onion and cut off ends to lay flat. Using a sharp knife, cut ⅔ of the way through the onion to quarter, then quarter again. Do not cut all the way through the onion; you just want to "flower" it.

Place the onion on heavy-duty aluminum foil, and add the rest of the ingredients. Wrap the onion with foil to seal in the flavors, and place it in a preheated 350° oven for approximately 50 minutes, or until the onion softens. When cooked, the dish will have a soft, velvety texture.

We serve 1 onion per person, and usually end up sneaking more from each other's plates. It's a great departure from the norm, and it couldn't be easier to prepare.

Side Dishes **51**

DIANE HODGES
South Holland, IL—WMBI

My version of broccoli salad has been well received at potluck dinners and by my family. The amounts given in my recipe are good for taking to a potluck, but the recipe can easily be cut down to serve fewer people. I would say that this recipe is relatively quick and easy to make and a pleasant way to get those veggies and fruits the experts tell us we should be eating.

Lemon Honey Broccoli Salad

Yield: 8-10 servings

8 cups chopped fresh broccoli
1 cup unsalted sunflower seeds (raw or roasted)
1 cup seedless raisins
1 cup mayonnaise
¼ cup (4 T) fresh lemon juice
2 T honey

In a large bowl (about 3 quarts) mix together broccoli, sunflower seeds, and raisins. Cover and refrigerate if you are not going to eat it right away. In a small bowl stir mayonnaise, lemon juice, and honey until smooth. Cover and chill dressing. Just before serving, add dressing to rest of salad and mix well.

VIRGINIA OLIVE
Cochrane, Alberta, Canada—KMBI

I am the mother of three almost-grown daughters. This recipe has become a family tradition for every Easter, Thanksgiving, and Christmas dinner since I discovered it about eight years ago. My girls and now my first son-in-law think it is the best. "Mom, are you making curried corn?" is always the question, and now they know the answer will always be yes. It is easy and quick, goes with any meat, and everyone loves it.

Curried Corn

2 lb. bag of frozen corn
½ cup margarine or butter, cut into small pieces
½ cup finely chopped onion or 2 T onion flakes
1 generous T curry powder (or more)
½–¾ cup sour cream
salt and pepper

Place first 4 ingredients together in a large pot on the stove. Heat gradually over low heat, stirring gently and frequently until margarine is melted. Simmer slowly for about 30 minutes or until corn and onion are soft. Stir frequently or it will stick. Gradually stir in sour cream, salt and pepper to taste, and more curry powder if you like. Heat through and serve immediately. I have also done it in the Crock-Pot. Simply put all ingredients (except sour cream) together and cook on low for 6–8 hours. It's a little easier but perhaps not quite as good. Add the sour cream right before serving. If you add it sooner, it might curdle.

JOANNE PANZETTA
Bushnell, FL—WKES

My daughter-in-law is of Greek descent and we both enjoy cooking. Heart-healthy.

Fasolakia
a Greek vegetable dish

¼ cup green olive oil
1 medium red onion, chopped
2 cloves garlic, minced
1 tsp. Cavender's Greek seasoning
¼ cup water
1 pkg. frozen, cut green beans
15½ oz. can diced tomatoes with garlic, basil, and oregano

In a large saucepan sauté in olive oil the onion, garlic, and Cavender's Greek seasoning. When cooked add the water, and cook for 5 minutes. Add green beans and stir occasionally over medium heat for 10 minutes. Add diced tomatoes and cook until green beans are tender, about 20–30 minutes.

DENISE R. SICKLES
Port Huron, MI—WNFA

This recipe is easy, yet looks complicated. It is a great comfort food and healthy! Kids like it even though it is vegetables.

Vegetable Casserole

2 cans (10 or 12 oz.) Veg-all (drained)
1 cup chopped celery
1 cup chopped onion
1 cup shredded cheddar cheese
1 cup mayonnaise (best if real, but OK if light mayo—not salad dressing)
1 cup sliced water chestnuts, drained and cut in half
1 sleeve of Ritz crackers, crushed

Mix everything together and put in 9x9" baking dish. Top with crushed Ritz crackers and pat with butter/margarine. Bake at 350° for 40 minutes.

Options: To make it a main dish, add 2 cups of cooked chicken breast or ham (chunked).

MILLY TORRES
Kissimmee, FL—WKES

Perfect Whole-Grain Rice

1 cup organic brown long-grain rice
3 cups water
1 T olive oil
1 tsp. salt

Put all the ingredients in a rice cooker, and you will enjoy delicious, fluffy rice.

SHIRLEY WITMER
Shippensburg, PA—WCRH

Quick and inexpensive. While I was working at Martin's Guest Home in Stony Fork, PA, Mr. Martin raised a crop of carrots, and had more than he knew what to do with. He told us to find as many recipes using carrots as we could. I came across this recipe for dilled carrots and decided to try it. The guests and employees at the guest home just loved it!

Dilled Carrots

4 T butter
1 tsp. chicken bouillon
½ tsp. dill weed
optional: ¼ tsp. salt
4 cups thinly sliced carrots

Melt butter in skillet; add bouillon and dill, stirring to blend. Add raw carrots, and stir to coat. Cover and cook on medium-high till carrots start to steam. Reduce to low heat and simmer till carrots are tender-crisp, about 10 minutes.

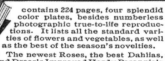

Soups and Salads

DEE BRESTIN
author of Friendships of Women
www.deebrestin.com

Table Talk: Questions for Rich Discussions

My daughter, Sally Brestin Hale, one of five Brestin children, says, "Every night at dinner my mother threw out a question, and we went around the table answering it. How profoundly those conversations affected my thinking and, therefore, my life. It's a rich tradition my siblings and I are continuing with our own families."

Here are some of our Brestin family dinner questions. These and more are also available to download from my Web site.

1. What was today's high point and low point?

2. What have you been thinking about a lot lately?

3. What observation can you make from today's proverb? (On 2/7 it would be Proverbs 2:7, or perhaps 12:7, or 22:7. If it didn't work, as on 9/30 there is no Proverbs 9:30, 19:30, or 29:30, we would say it was a Psalm 119 day and we'd look at Psalm 119:30 or even Psalm 119:130.)

4. What is one thing you appreciate about the person on your right?

5. On Thanksgiving Day: What are you thankful for this year that you could not have been thankful for last year?

6. During Advent, take a Christmas carol line by line and ask for observations.

7. I spy! Between Ash Wednesday and Easter (and often other times as well, because it led to such exciting discussions), we adopted a practice we learned from a radio program then in existence called *The Chapel of the Air*. Like the game of hide-and-seek, we taught the children to try to "spy" God during the week. There were four ways they might "spy" Him.

    1. An answer to prayer

    2. Unusual circumstances or timing, making you suspect God at work

    3. Unexpected grace

    4. God's help to do His work in the world

Dee's Spinach/Fruit Salad

To delight the eyes, palate, and waistline!

fresh spinach
fresh raspberries or sliced strawberries in season (mandarin oranges when berries not in season)
crumbled feta or goat cheese
optional: sliced almonds, or, to make it a meal, grilled chicken slices
lite raspberry vinaigrette dressing or lite poppy seed dressing

Toss gently together in any proportion you like, add dressing, and serve.

DANNA DEMETRE
author of Scale Down
www.dannademetre.com

❧ Come to the Table ❧

Ⅰn years past, the daily chore of planning and preparing dinner was more of a burden for me than a joy. It was one of my expected roles within our family that I readily accepted, but rarely cherished.

Recently, my husband, youngest son, and I moved to a place we fondly call "Switzaly" on the Swiss-Italian border in the quaint city of Lugano. Living in Europe has turned my old attitudes about cooking and mealtime upside down.

Whenever we dined in a local *trattoria*, *grotto*, or *ristorante* we noticed that the entire experience moved very slowly. In fact, once you occupy a table, it is considered yours for the entire evening. We realized over time that the server will never bring the check without being asked—to do so would be considered extremely rude.

Although we love all the tastes and smells of our new home, eating out is extremely expensive in Switzaly. And fast food, take-out, and home delivery are essentially nonexistent. So, as a result, I find myself cooking more than I have in decades . . . almost every single night! More important, we are "coming to the table" with a new attitude—as if we were having special company. We find ourselves lingering long after the last bite is swallowed. With candles lit and soft music playing, we share the details of our day and a few words from our new Italian vocabulary. We also tell how God has worked in the details of our day. And we marvel at how our new life in a new land has finally slowed us down enough to celebrate life.

As you try the fabulous recipes in this book, I encourage you to slow down, light a candle, and enjoy each mealtime as if you were dining with the Lord.

Nutty Barley Bake

6 servings

1 medium onion, chopped
1 cup medium pearl barley
½ cup slivered almonds or pine nuts
¼ cup butter
½ cup minced fresh parsley
¼ cup thinly sliced green onions
¼ tsp. salt
⅛ teaspoon pepper
2 cans (14½ oz. each) beef broth
optional: additional parsley

In a large skillet, sauté the onion, barley, and nuts in butter until barley is lightly browned. Stir in the parsley, green onions, salt, and pepper.

Transfer to a greased 2-quart baking dish. Stir in broth. Bake, uncovered, at 350° for 1¼ hours or until the barley is tender and the liquid is absorbed. Sprinkle with parsley if desired.

Bok Choy Salad

1 bunch small bok choy
1 bunch green onions (sliced)
1 pkg. shredded cabbage

Crunchies

2 pkgs. crumbled Ramen noodles
½ cup sesame seeds
1¾ cups of slivered almonds

Dressing

¾ cup salad oil (your choice of oil—coconut oil is the healthiest at high temps)
⅓ cup sugar (or honey for a healthier choice)
¼ cup white wine vinegar
2 T soy sauce (use low sodium for a healthy alternative)

Sauté bok choy, green onions, and slaw until brown in ½ cup butter and 2 tablespoons sugar. Stir constantly. Lay out on paper to cool. Add crunchies and dressing just before serving. (Makes enough for 2 salads.)

NANCY LEIGH DeMOSS
author of Choosing Forgiveness
www.reviveourhearts.org

A Gracious Host

When you think of an exceptionally hospitable host, does God come to mind? Psalm 23:5 portrays God as a gracious Host welcoming us to His home and table:

You prepare a table before me in the presence of my enemies . . .

The previous verse speaks of walking through "the valley of the shadow of death" (literally, "the valley of deep darkness"). We sometimes find ourselves in perilous places—but our Good Shepherd walks with us through those valleys—and on the other side a "feast" awaits us!

Charles Spurgeon used a wonderful word picture to describe the scene in this verse. God prepares a table carefully . . . just as a servant does when she unfolds the damask cloth and displays the ornaments of the feast on an ordinary peaceful occasion. Nothing is hurried, there is no confusion, no disturbance, the enemy is at the door; and yet God prepares a table, and the Christian sits down and eats as if everything were in perfect peace. Oh! The peace that Jehovah gives to His people, even in the midst of the most trying circumstances!

You may be surrounded by various enemies: something from your past that haunts you, people who would harm you, sickness, old age and death, your flesh, or Satan himself.

Will you choose to focus on your enemies or on your Host? Enemies will always lurk nearby, but you don't have to be overcome by them. Your Host will supply your needs and grant abundance in the face of opposition and danger.

The day is coming when all our enemies will be forever banished—no more night, no more sin, no more death, no more sorrow. In the meantime, you may feast with Him at the table He has prepared for you—in the presence of your enemies.

Due to the demands of hosting a daily radio program, speaking, and book deadlines, I do almost no "real" cooking and would have been hard-pressed to come up with a favorite recipe from my own kitchen! However, I have often been blessed by others who have ministered to me with tasty, home-cooked dishes. This soup recipe is one of my favorites, occasionally made for me by a dear friend who drops it by my home when I am holed away in my study. The soup is a blessing—but the friendship and hospitable heart it represents mean even more!

Tomato Basil Soup

1 T olive oil
1–2 medium onions, diced
5 cloves garlic, chopped
3 14 oz. cans crushed tomatoes
1½ T dried basil
2 tsp. dried oregano
1 tsp. dried thyme
2 cubes chicken bouillon
4 cups heavy whipping cream
salt and pepper to taste

Sauté onion and garlic in olive oil until onions are soft. Add tomatoes, basil, oregano, thyme, and bouillon cubes. Cover and simmer 10 minutes. Gradually stir in whipping cream and heat until piping hot. Season with salt and pepper.

Peter-John Campbell
MBN engineer

This is my sister Melissa's recipe for potato soup. It's one of my favorite things to make on a cold day.

Melissa's Easy Potato Soup

4 T (¼ cup) butter or margarine
1½ cup diced onions
4 cups diced potatoes
1 or 2 carrots, coarsely grated
2 cups water
½ tsp. pepper
1 tsp. dried dill weed
3 cups milk
2 T chopped fresh parsley
optional: instant potato flakes or buds

In a large saucepan, melt butter, and sauté the onions until golden. Add potatoes, carrots, water, salt, pepper, and dill weed. Bring to a boil; reduce heat to low, simmer until potatoes are tender; about 25–30 minutes. Stir in milk and parsley. Heat until hot.

For thicker soup, stir in instant flakes or buds during the last few minutes of cooking.

Mark Elfstrand
host on Mornings, WMBI

I remember having this salad at a friend's house years ago, but when I wanted to duplicate it, I had to search high and low. I finally found it on the Internet, along with quite a few variations. But for the past several years now, this one has been the family favorite. As a matter of fact, the recipe page is spattered with strawberry juice! This could easily qualify as a dessert as well as a salad.

Strawberry Pretzel Salad

Crust
2 cups crushed pretzels
¾ cup (1½ sticks) butter, melted
¼ cup sugar

Mix well and press into a 9x13" glass pan. Bake at 400° for 8 minutes. Allow to cool completely before proceeding with rest of recipe.

Filling
8 oz. cream cheese, softened
1 cup sugar
1 medium-sized Cool Whip

Whip together the cream cheese and sugar until very smooth. Fold in the Cool Whip. Spread on top of the cooled pretzel crust. Refrigerate while preparing the next layer.

Topping
6 oz. box of strawberry (or raspberry) gelatin
2 10 oz. boxes of frozen sliced strawberries (or raspberries) in syrup
2 cups boiling water

Dissolve the gelatin in boiling water. Add the frozen strawberries. (The water will melt them, and the frozen strawberries will start the gelling process.) Let stand for 10 minutes. Pour mixture onto cream cheese layer. Cover with plastic wrap and refrigerate for at least 2 hours.

Decorating ideas: Cut into equal portions (squares) and serve on a red lettuce leaf. At Christmastime, Sam's Club often has pretzels in the shape of evergreen trees. Put a dollop of whipped topping on each serving and "plant" a tree in the top. I hope you like it as well as the Elfstrands do!

CHRIS SEGARD

Midday Connection engineer

This fruit salad has become an annual Christmas favorite at the Segard home. The key is the fresh pineapple and that cinnamon glaze.

Christmas Fruit Salad

Yield: 6–8 servings

1 fresh pineapple, peeled and cut into pieces
3 oranges, peeled and sliced
3 kiwi, peeled and sliced
¼ cup pomegranate seeds or dried cranberries
optional: Star fruit or jicama slices cut with a
    small star-shaped cookie cutter are a festive
    addition.

Mix salad, place in large serving bowl, and gently toss with Orange-Honey Dressing.

Orange-Honey Dressing

¼ cup orange juice
¼ cup honey
½ teaspoon ground cinnamon

Shake all ingredients in a tightly covered container.

Recipes from Midday Connection Listeners

TORI ALBERTSON

Rock Island, IL—WDLM

Tori's Stuffed Green Pepper Soup

1 lb. ground beef
1 medium onion
6 cups water
4 beef bouillon cubes
1 (28 oz.) can diced tomatoes with liquid
1 cup instant rice
1 tsp. salt
¼ tsp. pepper
¼ tsp. paprika
2 medium sweet peppers, seeded and chopped

Cook meat and onion till browned. Drain well. Add bouillon cubes, tomatoes, seasonings, water. Bring to boil; reduce heat; simmer covered ½ hour. Then add the rice and cut-up peppers, and cook uncovered 10 to 15 minutes.

CAROLYN BELL

Pompano Beach, FL—WRMB

This fruit salad is easily made by using canned fruit, or if you have time you can use fresh fruits. It has been a tradition in our family to serve this along with our mother's famous Sour Cream Pound Cake. Usually it is made for holidays, but our family enjoys it any time of the year. My dear mother always comes to my mind when I take out my handwritten recipe that is on the old and stained index card I have used for so many years. Heart-healthy.

Cold Fruit Salad

2 eggs
⅓ cup sugar
1 large can of fruit cocktail, drained (fresh fruit
    makes it better if you have the time)
1 large can crushed pineapple (separate and
    save juice)
¼ cup lemon juice (2 lemons)
6–8 bananas

Beat eggs for 5 minutes. Add sugar, ¼ cup pineapple juice, and lemon juice. In a small saucepan cook mixture on low until it is thick. Cool mixture. Slice bananas while it is cooling. Pour the cooled sauce first over the sliced bananas, then over the rest of the fruit you have drained. This makes a large amount of fruit salad and looks great served in a clear glass bowl.

SUZANNE CONN

Fostoria, OH—WPOS

I like this salad because it's healthy, looks good, and tastes good. I eat a salad every day, and it has a nice variety from the food pyramid.

Cabbage Fruit Salad

4 cups shredded cabbage
2 oranges, peeled and cut into bite-sized pieces
2 red apples, chopped
1 cup seedless red grapes, halved
⅓ cup chopped pecans, toasted

Dressing

½ cup canola mayonnaise
¼ cup milk or unsweetened soy milk
1 T apple cider vinegar
¾ T raw honey

In a large bowl, toss cabbage, oranges, apples, and grapes; cover and refrigerate. In a small bowl, combine mayonnaise, milk, vinegar, and honey; cover and refrigerate. Just before serving, stir dressing and pecans into salad. Note: This dressing can also be used with shredded cabbage and some shredded carrots for coleslaw.

JEAN CARLEN
Deer Park, WA—KMBI

This recipe is delicious and also good for you! It's originally from my niece. An especially good one to take to women's potlucks.

Bean and Barley Salad

Makes 6-8 servings.

1 cup pearl barley
1 can red kidney beans, drained (or black beans)
2 carrots, finely chopped
2 tomatoes, seeded and chopped
¼ cup green onions, chopped
¼–½ cup chopped fresh parsley
2 T grated parmesan cheese
4 oz. crumbled feta cheese
optional: ½ cup cooked wild rice

Dressing
⅓ cup red wine vinegar
1 clove garlic, minced
½ tsp. cumin
1 tsp. salt
½ tsp. pepper
½ cup olive oil

Cook barley according to package directions, until tender but firm. Drain and rinse with cold water. Place in serving bowl. Add the rest of the ingredients and stir lightly to combine. Separately, with a wire whisk, combine vinegar, garlic, cumin, salt, pepper, and olive oil. Toss gently with bean/barley mixture.

ROSE DECHANT
Girard, OH—WCRF

This is quick and easy and a healthier option than canned soup. The colorfulness is inviting when there is a chill in the air. It is delicious served with ciabatta bread and can be a light meal in itself.

Not all my kids are crazy about spinach, but my husband and I enjoy it—and two out of four kids!

Tortellini Soup

Makes 6 servings.

2 cloves of garlic, crushed
1 T margarine
2 (13¾ oz.) cans of chicken or beef broth
    (College Inn recommended)
1 (8 oz.) package fresh or frozen cheese
    tortellini—thawed (I use tricolor and add it
    frozen—just simmer 5–7 extra minutes, but
    do not overcook)
1 (10 oz.) package fresh or frozen spinach—
    thawed (I prefer fresh)
1 (16 oz.) can diced, stewed tomatoes, undrained
grated Parmesan cheese (to taste)

In large saucepan over medium heat cook and stir garlic in margarine for 2–3 minutes. Add broth and tortellini; heat to a boil. Reduce heat; simmer 10 minutes. Add spinach and tomatoes; simmer an additional 5 minutes. Serve topped with parmesan cheese.

KATHLEEN DYRDA
West Chicago, IL—WMBI

This recipe is a family favorite. From May through October, this is the recipe I am requested to bring to gatherings and parties and to serve to company. It is quick, easy, and a tasty way to get my children to eat vegetables!

Broccoli Salad

2 bunches broccoli florets (some stems OK)
1 small red onion, chopped
1 cup peanuts (any kind)
6 slices cooked bacon, crumbled
½ cup mayonnaise (regular or light—must
    be mayo)
¼ cup sugar
1½ T red wine vinegar

Toss broccoli, onion, peanuts, and bacon together in a bowl. Mix together mayo, sugar, and vinegar. Pour over broccoli. Chill at least 1 hour before serving.

JULIE EICHEL
New Philadelphia, OH—WCRF
(also listen on the Internet)

This recipe is easy and delicious! My kids also enjoy eating it. I believe it's heart-healthy.

Bean Salad

1 cup sugar or Equal sweetener
1 cup red wine vinegar
1 cup olive oil
1 tsp. dried basil
2 T dried parsley
1 tsp. dry mustard
chopped onion (small pieces)
chopped red or green pepper (small pieces)
5 cans of beans—I like garbanzo, red beans, black beans, black-eyed peas, and kidney beans.

Mix first 6 ingredients together in a large bowl. Add onions, peppers, and beans. Mix well. Best refrigerated overnight. Serve as a bean salad or with tortilla chips.

MARIA HARDY
Tuscaloosa, AL—WMFT

A quick and easy chowder that my family enjoys eating on cold nights. I enjoy preparing it because it is so simple!

Corn Chowder

1 (28 oz.) can whole new potatoes, drained and diced
32 oz. creamed corn
1 T butter
½ cup chopped onion
¼ cup chopped green pepper
1 can cream of mushroom soup
4–6 cups milk (depending on how thick you like your chowder)
bacon bits and shredded cheddar cheese for topping

Melt butter or margarine. Sauté onions and green pepper in butter until soft. Add remaining ingredients and heat gently until thoroughly warmed. (Do not boil.) Top with bacon bits and cheese if desired. Serve with corn bread or a crusty loaf of bread.

DEANNA GAGALIS
Glenview, IL—WMBI

I found the recipe at Christmastime last year in the Gooseberry Patch Cookbook, Comfort and Joy, *and it has been adapted for this book. It's a healthy one. Every time I serve it, everyone wants the recipe! I've served it at gatherings in church and home. A light fruity salad that looks so pretty in a sparkling glass bowl.*

"Must Have Recipe" Salad

Serves 8–10.

2 5-oz. pkgs. romaine lettuce (or fresh spinach)
1 cup shredded Swiss cheese
⅓ cup sweetened, dried cranberries
1 cup cashews
1 apple, peeled and diced
1 pear, peeled and diced

Combine all ingredients in a large serving bowl; toss to mix. Pour salad dressing over salad and toss.

Dressing

¾ cup sugar
½ cup lemon juice
1 T red onion, finely chopped
1½ tsp. salt
¾–1 cup oil
1½ T poppy seed

Combine sugar, lemon juice, onion, and salt in blender container; cover and blend well. While blender is running, add oil in a slow, steady stream; blend until thick and smooth. Add poppy seed and blend an additional 10 seconds to mix.

CINDA D. KAUFFMAN
Shippensburg, PA—WCRH

In the summer, we grow our own squash and zucchini, so I enjoy making this soup for my husband, who had a heart attack approximately 1½ years ago. Everything in this soup is good for your health!!

Summertime Soup

approx. 4–5 lbs. of squash and/or zucchini
   (washed but not peeled, cut bite-sized)
1 large onion, chopped to your liking
2–3 cloves of garlic, chopped or minced
salt and pepper
2 16 oz. cans of petite cut diced tomatoes
   (zesty style)
2 cans of water
2 16 oz. cans of cannellini beans (drained)

I use a medium-sized granite roasting pan. Add zucchini, onion, garlic, salt, and pepper to pan. Pour the tomatoes over the top and then add water. Bake at 350° for approximately 1 hour, 15 minutes. Remove from oven and stir cannellini beans into mixture. Ready to eat!

PAMELA LEITMA
Hagerstown, MD—WCRH

I was asked to help out with a pastor's prayer luncheon at my church (Black Rock Bible Church). This is the hearty soup I came up with. It is kid-friendly (I have five kids who love it), heart-healthy, quick, and inexpensive.

Pam Leitma's Hearty Lentil Soup

2 cups lentils
2 T olive oil
1 14 oz. can diced tomatoes
4½ cups water
1 large chopped onion
1 stalk chopped celery
⅛ tsp. cumin
¼ tsp. oregano
1½ tsp. salt
1 cup diced ham
1 clove minced garlic
¼ tsp. basil
¼ tsp. paprika
3 T beef bouillon
salt and pepper to taste

Sort and rinse lentils. In large saucepan, heat oil. Stir in onion, celery, garlic, and ham, and cook until tender. Add lentils and remaining ingredients. Bring to boil. Reduce heat, cover and simmer until lentils are tender and soup gets thick, about 45 minutes. Add more hot water if necessary. Serve with warm bread and side salad.

Hint: To make it richer, you can substitute chicken broth for the water.

KELLY LONGHI
Valparaiso, IN—WMBI

My family loves this recipe because you sort of design your own. We put the garnishes into separate bowls and let everyone add what they like to the broth to create their own soup! All three of my children enjoy it, but my seventeen-year-old daughter especially loves it. She requests it for her birthday dinner. I usually make extra sautéed tortillas, because they are so good.

Tortilla Soup
Makes 12 1-cup servings.

1 T olive oil
4 corn tortillas, cut into ¼-inch wide strips
½ cup chopped onion
4 garlic cloves, minced
1 jalapeño pepper, seeded and chopped
1 16 oz. can diced tomatoes with juice
1 T ground cumin
2½ quarts (10 cups) strained chicken stock or
    unsalted canned chicken broth
salt and freshly ground pepper to taste
Garnishes: chopped avocado, shredded cheddar
    cheese, chopped cilantro, cooked and
    chopped chicken breast, and additional
    sautéed corn tortilla strips

In skillet, heat the oil and sauté the tortilla strips until slightly crisp. Place the onion, garlic, and jalapeño in a food processor, and process until ground. Stir into the tortilla mixture and sauté, stirring frequently, for 10 minutes. Stir in the tomatoes and cumin. Bring the mixture to a boil; then reduce the heat, cover, and simmer 15 minutes. Stir in the chicken stock and simmer 10 minutes more. Season with salt and pepper. Puree the soup in a food processor or blender in batches until smooth. Serve topped with desired garnishes.

GAY MARTIN
Oquawka, IL—WDLM

*This recipe was given to me by my husband's sister, now deceased. It was the one recipe that **every** member of our family loved!*

Seven Layer Jell-O

4 pkgs. Jell-O (lime, lemon, orange, strawberry)
hot and cold water
2 cups milk
1 cup sugar
1 pint (2 cups) sour cream
2 envelopes Knox gelatin
2 tsp. vanilla

Dissolve 1 pkg. lime Jell-O in 1 cup boiling water. Add ½ cup cold water. Pour into 13x9" pan to set. Bring 2 cups milk to boil; add 1 cup sugar, mix till dissolved. Dissolve 2 pkgs. Knox gelatin in ½ cup cold water. Add to milk and sugar mixture. Add 2 cups sour cream and 2 teaspoons vanilla. Beat well till blended. Set aside to cool. When lime Jell-O is set and mixture is cool, pour 1½ cups white mixture on set lime Jell-O. When mixture is set (using same directions for Jell-O and allowing layers to set), add lemon Jell-O, then white, then orange Jell-O, then white again, and strawberry Jell-O. Layers usually set up in about 15–20 minutes. Salad is very light, and pretty when cut.

PAULA P. MARTIN
North Augusta, SC—WLPE

This is a recipe from my mother-in-law, Ruth Martin, of Greenwood, SC. It is heart-healthy, quick, inexpensive, and serves at least 8–10 people.

Ramen Noodle Salad

2 pkgs. chicken-flavored ramen noodles
    (set flavor packet aside)
1 12 oz. bag broccoli slaw
2 bunches green onions, chopped (tops only)
1 cup of sunflower seeds (without shells)
½ cup of sliced almonds

Dressing

⅓–½ cup of red wine vinegar
½–¾ cup of vegetable oil (I use extra virgin
    olive oil)
optional: up to ½ cup of sugar
chicken-flavored packets from the noodles

Crush noodles in package. (I use a rolling pin.) Combine the broccoli slaw mixture, except almonds, in a large mixing container. Combine the dressing; add the dressing to the broccoli slaw mixture, stir well, and top with almonds. Can be made ahead and chilled. Stir well before serving.

GEORGIA NORDWALL
New Lenox, IL—WMBI

I devised this salad less than a year ago when I was trying to put together something healthy for my husband, recently diagnosed as being diabetic. Since that first day, my husband regularly asks for it. We have averaged fixing this 4–5 times per week, and have seen a marked improvement in many aspects of our health. When I serve it to others, they want more and ask for the recipe. It is good as a meal for 3–4 people, or taking to a buffet, it feeds many. I try to keep the ingredients on hand. This quick salad only takes 15–20 minutes to prepare. Because of the mandarin oranges and the crunchy texture, it tastes very good without salad dressing.

Heart-Healthy Colorful & Crunchy Salad

3 cups lightly chopped baby spinach
2 cups lightly chopped romaine lettuce hearts
1 cup chopped shredded carrots
1 cup chopped red cabbage
16 oz. mandarin oranges, drained

Top individual servings with sunflower seeds and "crumbled" cheese (not shredded, it tends to melt). I don't add the fruit until ready to serve. This salad stays fresh for a couple of days.

Variations, depending on tastes, needs, dietary prohibitions:

⅓ cup sliced almonds or chopped pecans
    or walnuts
tuna, with lemon pepper
grilled chicken
1 cup cooked macaroni
1 16 oz. can white or dark beans
½ cup chopped cucumber
½ cup chopped celery
½ cup chopped onion
½ cup bell pepper
chopped tomatoes
sliced strawberries

NANCI PECK
Coeur D'alene, ID—KMBI

My mother-in-law, Thea, shared this recipe with me; whenever I make it, I smile and remember to pray for her. She's an incredible mother to my husband and me. A quick recipe to make!

4-Bean Salad

1 can green beans
1 can kidney beans
1 can garbanzo beans
1 can yellow wax beans
1 small green pepper, sliced
1 small red onion, sliced

½ tsp. pepper
1 tsp. salt
⅔ cup vinegar
¾ cup sugar
⅓ cup salad oil

Drain and combine cans of beans. Add rest of ingredients. Mix everything together; put in container. Chill for at least 1 day for the best flavor, stirring occasionally.

VIRGINIA ROWLAND
Longview, TX—KGLY

I call this salad my "Funeral Salad." Actually, I have been called to take many dishes of it because people like it so much. This is the only salad I know made with lettuce that includes the dressing that does not ruin or get soggy if kept in the refrigerator; it will keep during the entire funeral occasion. I have taken it to potlucks and birthday parties also. It is absolutely delicious and has been a blessing to many people. Easy to make.

24-Hour Salad

1 head fresh green leaf lettuce (torn or chopped)
1 cup sliced green onions and tops
1 cup thinly sliced celery
1 can (8 oz.) water chestnuts, thinly sliced

Salad Dressing

2 cups Miracle Whip dressing or mayonnaise
1 T sugar
½ tsp. salt
½ tsp. pepper
2 cups shredded mozzarella cheese
½ cup Parmesan cheese

Layer salad ingredients in 9x13" dish in the order listed. Mix dressing and spread it over top of salad. Cover with plastic wrap. Refrigerate.

JOYCE SNADER
Pollocksville, NC—WLGP

This is a great inexpensive soup that tastes creamy and is warming to the tummy. Not hard to make and not time-consuming. Just as good the second day as the first.

Broccoli Wild Rice Soup

Yield: 8 servings

1 pkg. (6 oz.) chicken and wild rice mix
5 cups water
1 pkg. (10 oz.) frozen chopped broccoli, thawed
 or 1 cup fresh chopped broccoli
1 medium carrot, shredded
1 tsp. dried minced onion or 2 T chopped onion
1 can cream of chicken soup
1 (8 oz.) pkg. cream cheese, cubed
optional: ¼ cup slivered almonds

In large saucepan, combine rice, contents of seasoning packet, and water, and bring to a boil. Reduce heat, cover, and simmer for 10 minutes, stirring once. Stir in the broccoli, carrot, and onion. Cover and simmer 5 minutes. Stir in soup and cream cheese. Cover and simmer until cheese is melted. Stir in almonds (if desired).

MARSHA YONAN
Carol Stream, IL—WMBI

This is one of my favorite recipes. It is easy to prepare and very healthy. I serve it during holidays or Bible study group.

Marsha's Strawberry Spinach Salad

12 cups bite-sized pieces spinach
2 cups strawberries, sliced
⅔ cups sliced green onions
2 cans (11 oz. each) mandarin oranges
¼ cup pine nuts or pecans

Orange-Honey Dressing

¼ cup orange juice
¼ cup honey
2 T vegetable oil
2 T Dijon mustard

Shake dressing in tightly covered container to mix. Toss dressing and remaining ingredients except the nuts. Sprinkle with the nuts.

Mrs. Joseph (Karen) Visocky
Shawano, WI—WRVM-FM

I can still see my mother, after nearly 60 years, preparing this salad for our family. We were picky eaters, my 3 brothers and I, when it came to "veggies," so this was one way Mom got us all to eat cabbage. And we all loved it! Also a full serving of fruit and soooo delicious and refreshing. Goes great with fish, as well as other seafood, instead of the standard cole slaw for a change (and with many other entrées).

When my husband and I pig out on shrimp or crab legs at home, this is the dish, and the only dish, I prepare with it. A complete meal in just two dishes. I also prepare it with many other meals. Goes well with most anything!

All ingredients are pretty standard pantry/refrigerator items; it is quick and easy to prepare. Could use packaged shredded cabbage/slaw if desired. The few carrot shreds in the prepackaged mix would only add to the dish.

Fruit Slaw

Yield: 6–8 servings

2–3 cups chopped cabbage, as coarse or
    fine as you desire
2 large bananas, sliced (or 3–4 small)
1 20 oz. can pineapple chunks, in juice;
    drain and reserve juice
1 red-skinned apple: Gala works very well
1 Golden Delicious apple
1 Granny Smith apple
Optional: ½ cup walnut pieces (pecans are
    good, too)

Dressing

¼ cup lemon juice (may use bottled, frozen,
    or fresh)
¼ cup granulated sugar
½ cup mayonnaise (or Miracle Whip)
¼ tsp. salt

Chill the cabbage, pineapple, and apples. Drain pineapple well, over a medium bowl. Slice bananas into the pineapple juice and stir to coat well. Allow to sit while you shred or chop cabbage. (This will help prevent the banana slices from darkening.) Drain banana slices; reserve juice. Chop/shred cabbage into a large bowl. Choose apples with smooth, clean skin so you do not have to peel them. Core and slice apples; cut into bite-sized pieces. Add them to the reserved juice and stir to coat well, then drain. (Again, this will help prevent the apples from darkening.)

Lightly toss the cabbage, pineapple, banana slices, and apple together. Add the walnut pieces, if desired. Set aside while you make the dressing.

Whisk together the dressing ingredients; pour over the cabbage mixture. Toss lightly; refrigerate about 30 minutes before serving. Toss again, to distribute dressing before serving.

Needs to be eaten within 24 hours because the banana and apple will eventually darken in spite of the juice soak.

Breads

Recipes from Midday Connection Guests

KENDRA SMILEY
author of Be the Parent
www.KendraSmiley.com

The Aluminum Table

The table is aluminum and a little wobbly—probably because it isn't new. We don't use it every day, just every day for a week, once a year. The aluminum table is the meeting spot for meals as the family camps at the river. "The river" is the Tippecanoe River in Indiana. "The family" is a conglomeration of brothers and sisters and moms and dads and grandpas and grandmas and aunts and uncles and cousins and second cousins "removed" so many times that it is hard to keep track. Everyone who gathers is somehow related to the original owners of the camping spot, the wooded area on a family farm bordered by the lazy, beautiful river.

We are sometimes more than 70 in number, ranging in age from the 87-year-old patriarch of the group to my soon-to-be-born grandchild. Why do so many folks choose to assemble in the middle of the woods year after year? The answer is simple—love of family and love of God's creation.

The aluminum table holds the feasts of the day for our family, and the biggest and best meal is always breakfast. The menu never changes. It's bacon, eggs, and pancakes, with pancakes in the starring role. Everything is cooked over the campfire on a big griddle with hecklers and cheerleaders watching each turn of the spatula.

I wonder if there will be campfires and griddles and pancakes in heaven. I *know* it is a gathering of the family, the family of God. This summer our family will once again gather at the river in Indiana. One day those who know the Lord will gather at the river that flows from the throne of God.

Then the angel showed me the river of the water of life, as clear as crystal, flowing from the throne of God and of the Lamb. (REV. 22:1)

River Pancakes

1¼ cups buttermilk
1 egg
2 T salad oil
1 cup sifted flour
1 T sugar
1 tsp. baking powder
½ tsp. baking soda
1 tsp. salt

Mix ingredients together and cook on a hot griddle.

BARBARA SMITH
author of Food That Says Welcome

Making Bread

*"I am the bread of life. He who comes to me will never go hungry,
and he who believes in me will never be thirsty."*
(JOHN 6:35)

Sometimes I wonder how many bags of flour I have bought in my life, how many rolls I have formed, and how many biscuits and muffins I have shared with others. My grandchildren love bread and strawberry preserves. I must admit, bread is also my personal favorite. I would rather have bread than dessert!

Bread making is an example of a craft that has been lost to modern conveniences. It's easy to get fresh bread from bread machines or gourmet stores, but the value of bread is lessened when you don't have to put much effort into making it.

When you are making bread, you can use part of the dough to create sweet rolls of different varieties and then freeze the rolls for another occasion or a gift. Bread itself makes a great gift. It is a way for me to respond to those who care about my family and me. For example, I am always inspired by two doctor friends who are now in health-related services. They still carry their black bags and spend their time off caring and praying for those who need them. Their hearts and ministry are in service to others. These friends have come to our home on a Sunday afternoon to care for us, and one of the best ways I know to thank them is with the gift of homemade bread.

I still bake homemade bread every week, not for Paul and me, but for occasions that arise—opportunities to give to the homeless, the sick, the bereaved, or the grandkids, who love it! Because bread takes hours to make, it expresses a love that only time invested in hospitality can convey. It is a simple pleasure. Offering homemade bread as a gift is a beautiful way to care for someone else.

Cinnamon Rolls

(My grandchildren's favorite) Yield: 18 rolls

1 package dry yeast
1¼ cups warm water, divided
¼ cup sugar
¼ cup vegetable oil
1½ tsp. salt
2½ cups flour (more if needed)
¼ cup butter, melted
cinnamon

Icing
1 cup powdered sugar (or more)
2 T butter, melted
2 T water

Mix yeast with ¼ cup warm water and let set for 5 minutes or until it bubbles. Combine yeast with sugar, oil, salt, and remaining water in mixer using dough hook. Add flour, 1 cup at a time, until dough is the right consistency. Cover mixture and let dough rise until doubled. Turn mixer on to punch dough down. Cover and let rise again. Remove dough from mixer.

Preheat oven to 350°. Roll dough on a lightly floured area; spread with butter and sprinkle with cinnamon. Roll up in jelly-roll fashion and cut into ¾-inch slices. Place in greased round cake pans and let rise until double. Bake 10 minutes or until lightly browned. Cool in pans 10 minutes before removing. Mix icing and drizzle over rolls.

ANITA LUSTREA
Host of Midday Connection

Years ago I won $1,000 in a recipe contest through the Chicago Tribune *with this recipe. It was a special contest around Christmas in which the winner could earn a trip home for the holidays. I threw together a recipe, making it up as I went along. Recipe writers had to use dates, molasses, yeast, and margarine, all name brands, because the sponsoring companies were paying the prize money. I made up the recipe, never tried it, and still haven't made it to this day.*

I was shocked when the Tribune *test kitchen contacted me and said I'd won second place and a thousand dollars! I asked them if the bread was good and they said, "That's why you got second place. It was really good!" I hope you like it.*

Anita Lustrea's Award-Winning Whole Wheat Date Bread

Makes two standard loaves

3½–4 cups flour
2½ cups whole wheat flour
2 packages yeast
1 T salt
1 cup milk
1 cup water
¼ cup molasses
¼ cup of honey
3 T margarine
1 egg, beaten
¼ cup finally chopped dates coated with flour

In large mixing bowl combine 1 cup of flour and the whole wheat flour, yeast, and salt. Mix well. In a saucepan heat the milk, water, molasses, honey, and margarine until warm. Margarine does not need to melt. Add to the flour mixture. Add egg and dates. Blend at low speed until moistened. Then beat at medium speed for 3 minutes. Add the rest of the flour to make firm dough. Knead on floured surface about 10 minutes. Place in greased bowl and let rise until doubled. Punch down and divide in half and shape into loaves. Put in greased pans and let rise. Heat at 375° for 35–40 minutes.

SHARYN BROWNING
Loxahatchee Groves, FL—WRMB

As a volunteer at WRMB's Share from the very beginning, I have enjoyed talking with listeners and Moody staff, getting to know the other volunteers, eating some great food, and even getting several of those wonderful recipes that become traditional favorites of my family. I received the handwritten recipe for "Sticky Cinnamon Buns" from a volunteer many years ago and have made this easy, delicious bread for many occasions.

It became especially memorable because it was part of our traditional family breakfast on Easter and Christmas mornings as our children were growing up. Now that they are grown and gone, they eagerly anticipate it when they come back for a visit. Thanks, Moody, for being such a conduit for blessings to our family!

Sticky Cinnamon Buns

1 bag frozen Bridgeford or Rhodes Rolls (24 ct.)
1 3-oz. pkg. butterscotch pudding (not instant)
1 stick margarine (or butter)
¾ cup brown sugar
½ cup pecans (or more, if desired)
1–2 T cinnamon

Lightly grease 9x13" pan with margarine. Spread pecans on bottom. Place frozen rolls on top. Shake dry pudding over rolls. Melt margarine and brown sugar, and pour over all. Sprinkle cinnamon over top. Cover and let rise overnight. Bake for 20–25 minutes at 350°. Invert immediately.

KAREN HIEB
Eden Prairie, MN—WMBI (over the Internet)

This recipe is special to me because it has been passed down from my maternal grandmother to my mother and then to me, and both of these precious women have now gone to be with our Lord. I've made it for years, and though I've experimented with other recipes for banana bread, my husband always wants me to make this one.

This recipe is extremely easy to make and, as I've noted in the name of it, it has never failed for me.

Grandma Lee's Never-Fail Banana Nut Bread

2 cups all-purpose flour
1 tsp. baking powder
1 tsp. salt
½ tsp. baking soda
1 cup sugar
½ cup shortening
2 eggs
1 cup mashed bananas (about 3 bananas)
½ cup chopped walnuts

Sift together flour, baking powder, salt, and baking soda. Set dry ingredients aside.

Cream together sugar and shortening. Blend in eggs one at a time, beating well after each. Stir in mashed bananas, and then blend in dry ingredients, followed by chopped walnuts.

Oil and flour a 9x5" loaf pan. Pour batter into the pan and bake for 350° for 60–70 minutes.

Cool bread before slicing.

ROCHELLE HOSTETLER
Millersburg, OH—WCRF

My husband loves anything made with pumpkin, and this bread is very moist, so it's a winner in our family!

Pumpkin Bread

1½ cups sugar	1⅔ cup flour
½ cup oil	1 tsp. baking soda
2 eggs (beaten)	½ T baking powder
½ tsp. salt	⅓ cup water
1 tsp. cinnamon	1 cup pumpkin

Mix everything and place in bread pan. Bake at 350° for 1 hour or until done. Lay foil on top for last ½ hour.

KATIE LEWALLEN
Dayton, OH—WEEC

My six-year-old twin boys (Trent and Tristan) wanted to help with this recipe and had fun in helping me make and then eat it. It was a truly bonding and fun cooking experience for all of us. I even took pictures for our scrapbook. Telling your kids you are going to bake a turtle really gets them interested. Being in the kitchen together also opens up doors to talk to one another about things other than cooking, such as Bible stories.

Turtle Bread

You've heard of the soup; now here is the bread— kid-friendly and inexpensive.

2 tsp. active dry yeast
1 cup warm water
2 tsp. honey
¾ tsp. salt
2 tsp. vegetable oil
2½ cups all-purpose flour
1 egg
2 tsp. water
green food coloring

Dissolve the yeast in warm water. Whisk in honey, salt, and oil. Slowly stir in the flour; as it becomes harder to stir, knead the dough onto a lightly floured countertop, and continue dusting the dough with flour. Knead the dough by folding and pressing with the heel of your hand. Continue to knead until the dough springs back when you lightly poke it with your finger.

Form dough into a ball and place in a lightly greased bowl. Dust dough with flour, cover with a clean towel, and let it rise in a warm place for 30 minutes. When it doesn't spring back to a poke, you know it has risen enough.

After the dough has risen once, punch it down and form balls for the shell (body), 6" round; the head, 3" round; and four legs, 2" ovals. Assemble on a greased baking sheet, and add a small amount of dough for the tail. On the shell, make a crisscross pattern with a butter knife (4 diagonals one direction, and 4 diagonals the opposite, crossing one another). Use 2 raisins for eyes. Cover with plastic wrap and allow to rise again for 30 minutes. Preheat oven to 375°.

Mix 1 egg with 2 tsp. water and a few drops of green food coloring. Spread with brush over dough, coating 2 to 3 times (coloring will be light). Bake for 25 minutes, or until golden brown. Serve warm. Awesome with butter or honey butter. Kids love it.

SANDEE LUSTER
Moline, IL—WDLM-FM

This is the first recipe my three adopted daughters and I made together soon after I became their foster mom in 1995. At the time, they were 4, 5, and 7 years old. In 1998 I was blessed to adopt them. They are now 16, 17, and 19.

The recipe is kid-friendly, quick, and inexpensive.

Easy Muffins

2 cups self-rising flour
2 cups completely melted vanilla ice cream

Be absolutely sure that the flour is self-rising and that the ice cream is completely melted—not just soft. Mix together and pour into paper-lined muffin tins. Bake at 375° for 8–12 minutes.

Variations: Add frozen blueberries. Use other flavors of ice cream like praline pecan or butter brickle.

DIANE MUSIL
Lyons, IL—WMBI

Bold autumn flavors of sweet potatoes, cranberries, and cinnamon give seasonal appeal to these golden muffins. They will bring families and friends coming back for more as a breakfast treat, afternoon snack, or at a fall festival brunch.

Cranberry Sweet Potato Muffins

Yield: about 1 dozen

1½ cups all-purpose flour
½ cup white sugar
2 tsp. baking powder
¾ tsp. salt
½ tsp. ground cinnamon
½ tsp. ground nutmeg
1 egg
½ cup milk
½ cup cold mashed sweet potatoes
¼ cup butter (melted)
1 cup chopped fresh or frozen cranberries
sugared cinnamon

Combine flour, sugar, baking powder, salt, cinnamon, and nutmeg. In a small bowl, combine egg, milk, sweet potatoes, and melted butter. Stir in the dry ingredients just until moistened. Stir in cranberries. Fill paper-lined muffin cups half full; sprinkle with sugared cinnamon. Bake at 375° 18–22 minutes or until muffins are tested done by a toothpick. Cool in pan for 10 minutes before removing to a wire rack.

BONNIE REEB
Muscatine, IA—WDLM and WMBI

I'm contributing this recipe because I use it weekly. It is quick, inexpensive, and husband- and guest-friendly. (Oh, the aroma of freshly baked bread!) When I was growing up in Chicago, my father was a professional baker. I learned to make bread from scratch, but soon became too busy, so I developed this recipe, and it soon became our favorite. It's started in the bread machine and finished in the oven.

Oatmeal Bread

1¼ cups warm-to-touch water
3 T honey or sorghum
1½ T oil
2½ cups bread flour
⅔ cup oats, quick or whole grain
1¼ tsp. salt
1 T dry yeast (or 1 package)

Place ingredients in bread machine in order given.

Start dough cycle for 1½-lb. loaf. When dough cycle is completed, punch down dough, and let rest in pan while you prepare a lightly floured surface on counter. Using rolling pin, lightly roll bread dough into an 8x12" rectangle. Roll up, starting from the smaller side. Place in greased 4x8½" bread pan. Let rise, covered in warm place ½ hour or until about 1 inch over top of pan. Bake in preheated oven, 350° for 30 minutes. Let cool in pan at least 30 minutes before removing. Store in plastic bag. Bread freezes well. Use sharp knife to slice.

Note: I sometimes skip the rolling-out part and just place punched-down dough in the greased bread pan and gently punch dough into place in the pan. The bread may not be a "perfect" shape, but it tastes just as great!

JUDITH SHARP
Oregon, OH—WPOS-FM

This recipe originated with my mother-in-law—she made it before we were married (forty-seven years in May). I have not seen a recipe just like it. It is not too sweet and makes a good snack. We take it on picnics or daytrips or eat it with some cream cheese as a dessert bread.

Boston Brown Bread

1½ cups raisins
1½ cups water
1 cup sugar
2 T butter
1 egg
2¾ cups flour

1 tsp. salt
1 tsp. baking soda
1 tsp. baking powder
1 T vanilla
1½ cups chopped walnuts

Put raisins in water; bring to boil, simmer 10 minutes, and set aside. Cream sugar, butter, and egg together. Mix dry ingredients; then add to the creamed mixture. Stir in the raisins with liquid; mix well. Add vanilla. Fold in walnuts.

Grease and flour four (4) 1-lb. clean empty vegetable cans (such as from green beans, corn, etc.). Fill each can half full of batter.

Bake at 350° for 30 minutes; reduce heat to 325°, and bake another 15 minutes.

Remove bread from cans soon after it comes out of the oven. Cool before slicing.

WENDY J. WILLIAMS
Lookout Mountain, TN—WMBW

This is a recipe my mother made and now I make it. These rusks are great for morning coffee. Similar to biscotti, it is great to dunk in coffee, as snacks for children, and for a teething baby to gum!

Scorpa, Scandinavian Rusks

3 eggs
1 cup sugar
1 cup olive oil
3½ cups flour
1½ tsp. baking powder
½ tsp. salt
1 T cardamom

Combine all ingredients; mix well. Divide dough into 3 loaves.

Sprinkle sugar on tops. Place on cookie sheet or bottom of a broiler pan. Bake 35 minutes at 350°. Remove from oven, slice loaves, and place slices back on cookie sheet. Sprinkle again with sugar. Return to oven, and bake 20 more minutes.

KAREN WORLEY
Northport, AL—WMFT

My family enjoys these easy and healthy muffins on weekend mornings, when our schedule is more relaxed and we can linger a bit over breakfast and conversation.

Good-Stuff Muffins

Yield: 1 dozen regular or 2 dozen miniature muffins

1 egg
2 T oil
1 cup milk
1 cup whole wheat flour
1 tsp. baking powder
1 cup self-rising flour
1 cup old-fashioned oats
½–¾ cup brown sugar (or white)
¼ tsp. nutmeg
¼ tsp. cinnamon

Preheat oven to 400°. Spray muffin tin with cooking spray.

In small bowl, beat egg well. Add oil and beat. Stir in milk and set aside.

In large bowl, stir together the whole wheat flour and baking powder; add self-rising flour and oats, and mix well. Stir in sugar, nutmeg, and cinnamon. Add liquid and stir until just moistened. Fill muffin cups about ⅔ full. Bake 17–20 minutes. Enjoy!

Variations: Banana-Nut: Add 1 mashed banana and ¾ cup chopped walnuts or pecans.

Blueberry: Gently stir in ¾–1 cup fresh or thawed blueberries. Omit nutmeg and cinnamon.

Orange: Substitute 1 cup orange juice for milk; add dried cranberries and nuts if desired.

MADE IN THE CUP AT THE TABLE

The Easier Kind of Coffee
—No Coffee Pot Needed

G. Washington's Coffee dissolves instantly in hot or cold water. Absolutely pure, delicious coffee always. Each cup to order.

All the preparing scientifically and perfectly done by Mr. Washington's refining process—which eliminates the woody fibre, chaff and waste.

Send 10c. for Special Trial Size.   Recipe Booklet Free.

G. Washington Sales Co., Inc.,
522 Fifth Avenue   New York

G. Washington's COFFEE
Originated by Mr. Washington in 1909

Fancy Strawberries
Bring Big Profits

PLANT the right kind and grow them in the right way. Allen's illustrated Book of Berries describes all the best varieties and tells how to grow them profitably for home use and local market, also for distant shipping. A complete guide—this 1917 Book of Berries. Send for it today—*free*.

The W. F. Allen Co.
90 Market St.
Salisbury   Maryland

Si muore troppo presto

In verità vi dico che la cura della **Pylthon** guarisce tutte le malattie dove non havvi duopo dell'opera di chirurgo. E' una cura miracolosa che purifica e rinforza il sangue. Tonifica e fortifica i nervi. Preserva da morte immatura, assicura a tutti una bella vecchiaia senza acciacchi. Cura completa **L. 5,90** franco dappertutto. Opuscoli gratis. Spedire richiesta all'**Anglo-American Stores, via Monte Napoleone 16, M. lano.** Si trova anche in tutte le primarie Farmacie.

CURA ESTERNA non prendansi rimedî per bocca

R. M. LAMBIE,
ALL KINDS OF
BOOK HOLDERS
THE MOST PERFECT
Dictionary Holder.
Send for Illustrated Catalogue.
39 East 19th St., N.Y.

WHITING-ADAMS
BRUSHES
ALWAYS SUIT – NEVER FAIL
ALL KINDS
FOR SALE EVERYWHERE

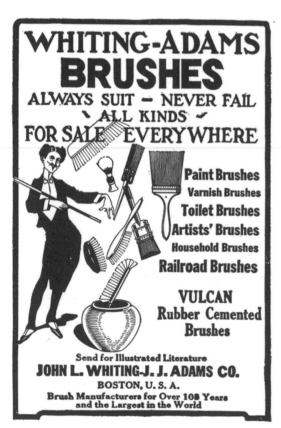

Paint Brushes
Varnish Brushes
Toilet Brushes
Artists' Brushes
Household Brushes
Railroad Brushes

VULCAN
Rubber Cemented
Brushes

Send for Illustrated Literature
JOHN L. WHITING-J. J. ADAMS CO.
BOSTON, U.S.A.
**Brush Manufacturers for Over 108 Years
and the Largest in the World**

A. J. REACH CO., LIMITED.
1022 MARKET ST., PHILA., PA.,
LEADING TENNIS OUT-FITTERS.

In shape our "**Taite**" Racket does not differ a **particle** from either the "**Beckman**" or "**Sears.**" In stringing, we claim superiority, as we use **Imported Gut only**, which by **actual test** stands 30 per cent. more strain than the American gut. We use the same **gut** in our **Quaker City Racket.** Send for our **Complete Tennis Catalogue.** In- and out-door **sports** of every description.

ALL STYLES
THE AMERICAN CYCLES
DESCRIPTIVE CATALOGUE
ON APPLICATION.
GORMULLY & JEFEERY
MFG. CO.
CHICAGO, ILL.
& PRICES   THE LARGEST MANUFACTURERS IN AMERICA

"AS YOU LIKE IT."
Installment Plan or **CASH.**
BICYCLES, TRICYCLES, VICTOR, VICTOR, JR., VICTOR SAFETY, SPALDING'S PREMIER. For full particulars address with stamp,

A.G. SPALDING & BROS.
**108 Madison St., Chicago,
241 Broadway, New York.**

Desserts

Recipes from Midday
Connection Guests

ROSALIE DE ROSSET

professor at Moody Bible Institute
and guide for the Midday Connection Book Club

Around the Table

When my siblings and I were growing up in Peru, South America, we ate together three times a day, seven days a week. As busy as my parents were—planting churches, teaching people to read, offering medical care, running Bible classes, visiting the nationals, running several church services a week, and homeschooling—mealtimes were sacred. Even after we were grown, when we were together at holidays or during summers in the United States, mealtimes were significant.

When my parents weren't with us, we were always with my grandmother. We gathered around her little oak table in her tiny apartment, eating a brown roast with potatoes and carrots, butterscotch pie or pineapple-walnut rolls, and lettuce salad with bananas and special dressing. I can still hear her scolding me for leaving an inch of coffee in my cup. She and my mother had lived through the Depression, and they never wasted anything.

Around those tables we caught up with the events of the day, laughed or fought heartily, attempted to solve problems, and were very connected with one another. It is a practice that has never ended; when my family is together, we eat together, three times a day.

My mother's apple dumplings are legendary—made of tart apples, never oversweetened, lightly tossed with cinnamon. I have been known to eat an embarrassing number in a few hours—still could—though these days it is easier for her to make a pie than dumplings. Here is the recipe according to my 92-year-old mother. (She goes by feel.)

Apple Dumplings

Make your favorite pie dough and roll it out in a big round, thin circle. Cut this in a series of rounds or squares that can be folded over half a cored apple (medium-sized and mellow—not superhard). Fill the center of the half apple with sugar and a little cinnamon, and wrap it in the dough. Lay the dumplings in your pan and bake them until golden brown (maybe 45–50 minutes—watch them) at 350–375°. My mother says you don't want a raw apple in a baked crust or a burnt apple in an underbaked crust. There you have it.

LOIS EVANS
author of Stones of Remembrance
www.loisevans.org

Memories on a Budget

This recipe was given to me as a student wife, during our seminary years in the 70s. We seminary wives were always looking for inexpensive ways to make our budgets work and still provide our families with delicious, wonderful, and appealing meals. Little did I know that this quick and easy dessert would become my family's favorite dessert over the years. So it is a testimony for me every time I make it and see what joy and happiness it brings to my family . . . and it also reminds me of how sweet it is to know and walk with the Savior in every season of life.

We made memories then, and now we are watching our children and grandchildren lingering around the dinner table, listening, telling stories, sipping coffee or milk, and eating cherry cake. I can't begin to number the lessons taught and lessons gained, characters built on stories of how God brought us over and is continuing to show Himself strong.

Many lessons taught about God's goodness for four generations have been shared around cherry cake.

It doesn't take a lot of money to pass on memories, a legacy, and a heritage. Sweet memories and sweet conversation with a sweet Savior have built our trust in Him. 'Tis so sweet to trust in Jesus.

Cherry Cake

1 pkg. yellow or white cake mix
½ cup oil
2 eggs
½ cup water
1 can pie filling—cherry, strawberry, etc.

Pour oil into 13x9" pan, tilting to evenly distribute on bottom. Add dry cake mix, eggs, and water. Mix well with fork for about 2 minutes. Clean sides and smooth cake mix over. Drop pie filling by spoonfuls evenly on top of mixture and swirl slightly with spoon.

Bake 35–40 minutes at 375°. Serve warm with or without ice cream or whipped cream. It is also good with powdered sugar sprinkled lightly on top.

TRACY GROOT
author of Madman
www.tracygroot.com

Christmas Eve Feast

I've always been enchanted by holiday traditions. When I married, I decided to create a tradition of my own. Since Jack's side of the family celebrated Christmas the Saturday before and my side met on Christmas Day, I invited anyone who wanted to come for a special Christmas Eve Feast.

Jack's parents and Jack's sister, Rita, along with Rita's family, came to the very first Feast. I planned the menu weeks ahead. I scrubbed the house to a spit-shine and happily fretted over the endless details incumbent upon a holiday hostess. It was important for that first Feast to go well, and it did. The guests were suitably impressed by the food, and the atmosphere was pleasant and festive.

One year I decided to serve prime rib. I investigated many methods of cooking it, and finally decided on the One True Way. With guests about to arrive, I prepared a final herb rub—and noticed a funny smell.

"Is that my *roast?*" I shrieked.

"Yes," Jack admitted, as if he'd noticed it for a while.

Turned out my prime rib was way past its prime—the meat was foul. Christmas Eve Feast was about to be a complete failure. Maybe my husband expected wails and groans—maybe I did. But many years of celebrating this Christmas Eve Feast taught me one thing: it isn't about the food, though the food is nice. It isn't about the atmosphere, though atmosphere is important. It's about people. It will always be about people.

"Stoke up the grill!" I hollered. "Meijers is open for another twenty minutes!"

I flew to the store, grabbed an armload of steaks, and made it home just as the first guests arrived.

It wasn't prime rib, but the most important feature to adorn that table was there—family.

This is special to me for two reasons: It's my son Evan's favorite dessert, and always requested for his birthday "cake," and it came from a dear friend, Amy Strating, whose recipes compile about half of what is in my recipe box.

Whopper Dessert

35 Oreo cookies, crushed
6 T butter or margarine, melted
1 half-gallon vanilla ice cream, softened
1 12 oz. box of Whoppers candy, crushed, reserving ¾ cup
1 jar of hot fudge topping (I use Mrs. Richardson's), very slightly warmed
1 8 oz. container of Cool Whip, thawed

Combine crushed Oreos and melted butter, and place in the bottom of a 9x13" pan. Mix ice cream with crushed Whoppers until well combined; then spread on Oreo layer. Freeze until firm. Spread with the jar of hot fudge topping, then the Cool Whip, and sprinkle with the reserved crushed Whoppers. Keep frozen until serving.

LIZ CURTIS HIGGS
author of Bad Girls of the Bible *and* Embrace Grace
www.LizCurtisHiggs.com

Setting Our Table Aglow

Our family dining room table was the color of split pea soup, and for good reason: Mother set it on fire. Not on purpose, of course; one December evening she left a candle centerpiece burning and came back to find the table ablaze. We kids thought it was pretty exciting (flames in the dining room!), but our mother simply doused the fire with water, then went to work salvaging our mahogany table.

The gaping hole in the center was repaired with wood filler; then she painted the whole table olive green and wiped the surface with a brown, streaky finish: a process called "antiquing," wildly popular during the late 1960s.

Was it the ugliest dining room table on the block? Boy, howdy. Did the strange color put a damper on our fun when the clan gathered for a meal? Not for a minute. Such tales, recounted with glee, only added to our growing collection of family stories, unpacked every Christmas right along with the decorations.

Though only one year featured a flaming table, each holiday the scent of baking gingerbread wafted through the house. My paternal grandmother made sure our cookie jar remained filled with soft, thick gingerbread cookies, lovingly cut out in the shape of a bell. Decades later, my siblings and I still use her recipe, bringing to our own Christmas tables plates of warm, freshly baked cookies: tart with the taste of dark molasses and sweet with the memory of Christmases past.

Grandma's Soft Gingerbread Cookies

½ cup (1 stick) butter
½ cup sugar
½ cup dark molasses
1 T cider vinegar
½ tsp. salt
½ tsp. cinnamon
1 tsp. ginger
½ tsp. baking soda, dissolved in a little
    hot water
1 egg
3 cups sifted all-purpose flour
1 tsp. baking powder

Boil first 7 ingredients in a saucepan until butter is melted and mixture is boiling rapidly. Stir in baking soda mixture; then cool for a few minutes. Add egg, flour, and baking powder, stirring as you go. Cool dough in saucepan in refrigerator for 1 hour. Roll out dough on floured board to ½" thickness. Cut in fun shapes. Bake in middle of oven at 350° for 8–10 minutes on greased cookie sheet. Store in closed container with soft bread.

LESLIE PARROTT
author of You Matter More than You Think
www.RealRelationships.com

What a Real Meal Will Do for Your Marriage

When you allow the fast-food mentality to infiltrate the majority of your meals, you are missing out on one of the very best means to reclaiming the moments you've been missing together. Why? Because a leisurely meal gives a couple an oasis of slowness and a way to rejoin their spirits. Think about it. What happens in your relationship when the two of you step off the treadmill to actually sit down without a scheduled appointment nipping at your heels? A meal where you don't hear or say things like: "We've got to order fast," or "We don't have time for dessert," or "We've got to eat quickly," or "Where's our waitress?" A slow meal occurs when you allow your souls to catch up and be reunited after a fast-paced day.

We recently celebrated our twentieth wedding anniversary. And like most couples, one of the ways we marked this milestone was with a fancy meal—just the two of us. But this was like no meal we had ever experienced. We arrived at the five-star herb farm in the foothills of the Cascade Mountains at 6:00 and the meal did not end until well after 11:00. No entertainment, no interludes, just five leisurely hours of a nine-course meal. Occasionally we took a walk around the gardens in between courses, but most of our time was spent talking about anything and everything that came to mind. Talk about having time to let your souls catch up! With our two boys safe at home with a babysitter, we relished the slow pace of the evening. We basked in the time we had with no agenda other than to be together.

Granted, this is not the kind of meal we'd want all the time. It was highly unusual, to say the least. But it underscored for us the value "slow food" brings to our relationship. Truth is, a slow approach to food strengthens any relationship. There is something in the nature of eating together that forms a bond between people. As Carl Honoré points out in his book *In Praise of Slowness*, "It is no accident that the word 'companion' is derived from the Latin words meaning 'with bread.'" Meals become meaningful when we share them with our spouse. Dining together relaxes our spirits and makes us more loving. It's what caused famed playwright Oscar Wilde to say, "After a good dinner one can forgive anybody, even one's own relations."

French Iced Coffee

A wonderful, slushy coffee drink!

3 cups strong coffee
2 cups sugar
1 pint cream or half & half
1 quart milk
2 tsp. vanilla

Dissolve sugar in hot coffee. Cool. Add other ingredients. Pour into milk cartons to freeze. Remove from freezer 2 hours before serving. Mix and serve very icy.

My mother-in-law kept this recipe secret for many years before finally sharing it with the many people who had asked for the recipe. Serve it as an elegant drink in a punch bowl.

NANCY SEBASTIAN MEYER
author of Beyond Expectations
and Talk Easy, Listen Hard
www.hope4hearts.net

A Grandmother's Touch

Although my grandmother is gone now, I remember her cracker pudding from when I was a little girl. Recently I visited my cousin, her only other grandchild, and we made this pudding together and enjoyed eating it while we reminisced about Grandma. Cracker pudding is definitely a "comfort food."

Old-Fashioned Cracker Pudding

2 cups milk
1 egg, separated
½ cup sugar
½ cup crumbled saltine crackers
⅓ cup shredded coconut
½ tsp. vanilla
¼ cup sugar

Scald milk in a saucepan; then turn down heat and add a mixture of the egg yolk, sugar, cracker crumbs, and coconut. Mix well and continue stirring until thickened (about 3 minutes). Remove from heat and stir in vanilla. Pour in 8x8" (or equivalent) baking dish.

Beat egg white until stiff and add sugar gradually as you continue beating to make a stiff, glossy meringue. Spread over pudding and put in a preheated 425° oven for 5 minutes or until browned. Refrigerate.

ETHAN POPE
author of Identity Theft
www.foundationsforliving.org

Foundations for Living

One of my favorite memories of growing up is eating cookie dough before my mom could bake the cookies. My mom had a special cookie recipe (see below) that required the baker to make the dough, roll it into a "log," sprinkle it with flour, wrap it in wax paper, and put it in the freezer to harden. The concept was that whenever you wanted to bake a few cookies, you could pull the cookie log out of the freezer, cut several slices off, and bake the cookies. The only problem was, I loved the cookie dough so much that I would eat it all before my mom could bake the cookies. (For health reasons, I don't recommend eating raw cookie dough like I did *and still do*, but to actually bake the cookies.) I have shared my love for making and eating cookie dough (and sometimes actually baking the cookie dough) with both of my children.

I find an interesting correlation between baking cookies and managing money. If you eat (or spend) all of the cookie dough before you actually bake the cookies, you will never have an opportunity to enjoy fresh-baked cookies (money) in the future. In so many cases, managing money is about delayed gratification. For example, if you want to purchase a home, you have to "save" for the down payment and not eat or "consume" every dollar before it goes into your money-market account. In the same way, you can't eat your cookie dough and have fresh-baked cookies later.

Have you ever noticed how much our culture correlates food to money? Dough, bread, bringing home the bacon, and bean counting, just to list a few expressions where food terms are used for money.

Ice Box Cookies
½ cup butter, softened
1 cup sugar
1 egg
2 tsp. vanilla
1¾ cups all-purpose flour
½ tsp. baking soda
½ tsp. salt
½ cup chopped pecans

Cream butter; gradually add sugar, beating well. Add egg and vanilla; beat well. Combine flour, baking soda, and salt; then add to creamed mixture, beating well. Stir in chopped pecans.

Shape dough into 2 long rolls, 1 inch in diameter. Sprinkle rolls with flour; then wrap the rolls in waxed paper, and chill for 2 hours or until firm.

Unwrap roll, and cut into ¼-inch slices. Bake on ungreased cookie sheet at 400° for 8–10 minutes.

JAN SILVIOUS
author of Moving Beyond the Myths *and*
Look at It This Way
www.jansilvious.com

If you dare, mix up the following dessert. Your boys and men will love it. At least my guys still do!

Chocolate Delight

1 cup flour
1 stick margarine
1 cup pecans, chopped
8 oz. cream cheese, softened
1 cup powdered sugar
1 large container Cool Whip
6 cups milk
1 large instant vanilla pudding
1 large instant chocolate pudding

Mix flour, margarine, and pecans well, and press into 9x13" pan. Bake at 350° for 20 minutes. Remove from heat and let cool. Mix cream cheese, powdered sugar, and 1 cup of Cool Whip. Spread over crust. Mix both puddings and milk; spread over the cream cheese mixture, making 1 layer chocolate and 1 layer vanilla. Top with the rest of the Cool Whip. Cover and chill for 2–3 hours before serving. As we say in the South, this is so good it makes you want to slap your granny!

KIM THOMAS
author of Potluck
www.kimthomasbooks.com

An Honest Little Cake

When I relinquished my baking duties to Jim, he took my chocolate sheet-cake recipe and made it his own. He did not attempt to adjust any of the measurements or ingredients; he merely reinterpreted the form of the cake. Instead of baking it as a stretched-out sheet cake, Jim stacks it high by baking it in two round 9" pans. That is what logical recipe followers are comfortable with adjusting, the part that has little effect on the flavor of the baked item.

Stacking a cake that was originally intended to be a sheet cake means that it rarely comes out perfect. It is usually lumpy looking, and the frosting lays like thin Lycra over less-than-tight abdominals. But it remains an honest little cake and holds its own against prettier ones. People will, in fact, fight their way to the potluck table for Jim's Ugly Chocolate Cake.

Searching my memory, I cannot remember anyone ever complaining, "If only the cake looked pretty, it would taste better!" Actually, an uneventful or disappointing evening at the experimental entrée table can be quickly forgotten with a bite of ugly but dependable chocolate cake. During one potluck, a carefully stylish and lip-glossed girl wore a chocolate-icing ring around her mouth from her encounter with the cake. The ring lingered long after the cake was gone, and when the girl smiled she looked vaguely like a sock monkey.

You can always count on Jim's cake to taste good each time he makes it. It's bona fide and dependably Jim's chocolate cake—and it's ugly. But it is a reminder that goodness is often hidden behind an imperfect exterior. Appearances of all kinds are welcome at the potluck. And we must never let a little "ugly" keep us from experiencing what is good.

Jim's Ugly Chocolate Cake

2 cups granulated sugar
2 cups all-purpose flour
4 T cocoa
2 sticks butter
1 cup hot water
½ cup buttermilk
1 tsp. baking soda
1 tsp. vanilla extract
2 large eggs

Preheat oven to 350°. Sift together sugar, flour, and cocoa in medium-sized bowl. Set aside.

In medium saucepan, bring butter and hot water to a boil. Pour over sifted ingredients and mix.

In a separate bowl, mix together buttermilk, baking soda, vanilla, and eggs. Stir into cocoa mixture and pour into 2 greased and floured 9" cake pans. Bake about 20 minutes, until inserted toothpick comes out clean. Allow to cool 20 minutes before frosting.

Icing

1 stick butter
4 T cocoa
⅓ cup milk
1 lb. powdered sugar

Bring butter, cocoa, and milk to a boil; then remove from heat. Add powdered sugar, mixing well until sugar is dissolved. Frost first layer of cake. Stack second layer on top and finish frosting entire cake.

Adapted from *Potluck*. Published by WaterBrook Press, Colorado Springs, CO, 2006 (used by permission).

LISA WHELCHEL
author of Creative Correction
www.lisawhelchel.com

Seasonal Colors

When we think of Christmas, we often paint a picture in our mind in strokes of green and red against a canvas of white, with a touch of silver and gold here and there. Who was the first artist to choose these hues from their palette? It was God. It is He who paints the seasons with colors. At Christmas, we have the green of evergreen trees and wreaths, the red of the poinsettia, the white of a snowman, and the silver of the stars and the gold of the trumpet on that hillside announcing Jesus' birth.

Think about it. What colors come to mind when someone mentions Easter? Azalea pink, lavender iris, buttercup yellow? The most common colors of springtime in bloom. The same is true for Thanksgiving, when we decorate with pumpkin orange, roasted-turkey brown, and maple-leaf red.

God uses the language of color to help His people understand eternal truths. " 'Come now, let us reason together,' says the LORD. 'Though your sins are like scarlet, they shall be as white as snow; though they are red as crimson, they shall be like wool' " (Isaiah 1:18).

Let the colors of each season remind us of the Master Painter and prompt us to thank Him for His creative use of color in our world.

Bowls of Color and Corn

Popcorn is always fun to make, and even "funner" to eat. Coat it with sugar and dye it with color, and that's the "funnest" of all!

16 cups popped popcorn
2 cups granulated sugar
½ cup light corn syrup
1 tsp. baking soda
1 tsp. salt
2 tsp. almond extract
paste **food coloring**

Spray the inside of a 14x20" cooking bag with nonstick cooking spray. Place the popped popcorn in the bag.

In a 2-quart microwave-safe bowl, combine the sugar and corn syrup. Microwave until the mixture boils, about 2 minutes; then stir and microwave for 2 minutes longer. Stir in the baking soda, salt, and almond extract. Tint the sugar mixture with the food coloring.

Pour the hot syrup over the popcorn in the bag; twist the top shut and shake until well coated. Microwave for 3 minutes, stirring and shaking after each minute.

Spread the popcorn out over a large sheet of aluminum foil that you've sprayed with nonstick cooking spray. Cool to room temperature; then transfer to an airtight storage container (that is, if there's any left after the neighborhood kids find out how cool the mom in your house is!).

Adapted from *The ADVENTure of Christmas*, Lisa Whelchel, Multnomah Publishers, 2004. Used by permission.

BECKY BORGSTROM
Boynton Beach, FL
administrative assistant at WRMB

This is the dessert I made every year for my son Eric's birthday. He preferred this to birthday cake. This dessert is kid-friendly, but adults love it. Also, it's quick to make.

Chocolate Éclair Dessert

Yield: 15 large servings

1 box graham crackers
2 regular boxes instant French Vanilla pudding mix
1 8-oz. Cool Whip
3¼ cups milk (lowfat or skim works fine)
1 can ready-made milk chocolate frosting

Blend both boxes of pudding mix with milk. Mix with electric mixer for 2–3 minutes at medium speed. Add container of Cool Whip, and mix at low speed until blended.

Place one layer of graham crackers (whole) on bottom of greased 13x9" pan. Pour ½ of pudding mixture on top of graham cracker layer in pan. Place second layer of whole graham crackers on pudding mixture. Pour the second half of pudding mixture on top of second layer of graham crackers. Top with third layer of whole graham crackers.

Chill in refrigerator for 2 hours. Frost with milk chocolate frosting. (Can be frosted without chilling, but it's easier when graham crackers are hard and chilled!)

Refrigerate for at least 6–8 hours before serving.

TRICIA BOYLE
MBN program producer

This is a family favorite that the five of us Boyle kids grew up making with my mom. It adds great color to any Christmas gathering, it is quick to make, and kids (and adults) enjoy making it. (It's kind of messy, though.)

Christmas Wreaths

Makes about 30 cookies

30 regular (large) marshmallows
½ cup butter
¼ tsp. green food coloring
¾ tsp. vanilla
3½ cups cornflakes
red cinnamon candies (red hots)

Melt marshmallows, butter, food coloring, and vanilla together. Stir well, being careful not to burn it. Add cornflakes, stirring well. Form into wreath shapes on wax-paper-lined cookie sheets. Drop red cinnamon candies onto wreaths.

Tip: The mixture is very hot. I generally use cold butter on my fingers to keep from burning them.

Mark Elfstrand
host on Mornings, WMBI, Chicago

Chocolate Chip Pecan Pie is an Elfstrand family holiday tradition. It is usually baked for Thanksgiving and Christmas. Served warm with ice cream, it makes for a quick "lights-out" at nap time.

Chocolate Chip Pecan Pie

2 eggs
½ cup flour
½ cup sugar
½ cup brown sugar
1 cup butter, melted
1 cup chocolate chips
¾ cup pecan halves

Beat together first 5 ingredients. Add chocolate chips and pecan halves. Pour into deep-dish pie crust. (Optional: With an extra ¼ cup pecan halves, decorate the top in spoke fashion.) Shield edge of crust with foil. Bake at 350° for 1 hour. (One never satisfies my family—I have to make two of them!)

"No-Fail" Pie Crust

1 cup flour
1 tsp. salt
⅓ cup butter-flavored Crisco
1 egg
1 tsp. apple cider vinegar
5 T very cold water

Measure dry ingredients. Cut in Crisco with pastry blender, or shake well in a sealed mixing bowl until small pea-sized balls form. In measuring cup mix egg, vinegar, and water. Mix well. Add half of liquid to flour mixture. Secure seal on bowl and swirl in a rolling motion until mixture adheres and forms a ball. If necessary, add 1 tsp. more of liquid at a time until mixture forms a ball. Roll onto a well-floured surface, into a circle to fit the size of your pie pan. Carefully roll the pastry around the rolling pin and lay the crust in the pie pan. After chocolate chip mixture is poured, crimp the edges of the crust as desired (with alternating thumb and forefinger, or by pressing with a fork). Keep crust covered and well chilled if not using immediately.

Kai Elmer
national music assistant for MBN

These recipes come with a little help from my grandmother, Evy Elmer, from Burlington, WA. My grandparents immigrated to the U.S. from Denmark after World War II, and I can't remember a Christmas dinner at their house when we didn't have Ris a la Mande for dessert. The best thing about Ris a la Mande, though, is that as part of Danish tradition, we always hide an almond in a bowl, and the lucky person who receives the almond in his or her serving wins a prize!

Christmas Rice Dessert

Julegrød is the base for Ris a la Mande, but can also be served alone hot. Sprinkle sugar and cinnamon over the porridge and put a pat of butter in the center of the porridge. I estimate the Rice Pudding recipe makes about 4-6 servings. As far as the Ris a la mande is concerned one cup of Rice Porridge along with the other indredients makes 6 servings of dellicious but rich ris a la mande.

Julegrød (Christmas Rice Porridge base)

2 cups rice
6 cups milk
1 cup heavy cream
1 tsp. salt

Cook rice in milk for approximately 1 hour in a heavy saucepan. Stir often with wooden spoon. Add more milk if porridge base gets too stiff. Add cream and salt when rice is done.

Ris a la Mande

1 cup rice porridge (from above recipe)
1 cup whipped cream
¼ cup chopped, blanched almonds
2 T sugar
1 tsp. vanilla extract
raspberry syrup, heated

Place the cold porridge in mixing bowl. Add sugar, chopped almonds, vanilla, and whipped cream. Mix well and chill. Drizzle warm fruit sauce on top to taste.

DONNA LELAND
host on WMBI

After making high-fat icing (Crisco, butter, cream cheese) for a few weddings, I began to feel guilty about feeding people such an artery-clogging mixture. So I prayed to the Lord about what to do for my next cake, and He allowed me to discover this alternative.

Low-fat Icing by Donna

Ices one 8-inch cake

1 small package instant pudding
¼ cup milk
1 small container whipped topping, thawed

Mix pudding and milk. If it is lumpy, add a couple of tablespoons milk till it is smooth. Gently fold in the thawed whipped topping. Use a big spoon or spatula to get the pudding off the bottom and gently incorporate into the topping. Gentle and slow mixing are the trick to this. Set the icing in the fridge for at least 15 minutes to set. You can use this in a piping bag and it stands up nicely. The flavor depends on which pudding mix you pick. My favorite is butterscotch.

ANITA LUSTREA
host & executive producer
Midday Connection

When I was young I spent many summers on my grandparents' farm. The noon meal on the farm was a personal favorite. Family and farmhands and whoever happened to stop by would sit together and chow down. It seems there was always room for one more to join in the feast. I learned true hospitality on the farm.

In the evening we played games and visited. Those were memorable table times. We laughed and talked and cried, and laughed some more. My cousin Jamey told stories that kept us in stitches. I learned how to listen and take turns at the table. My life was shaped by every person who joined us at the table, whether they were parents, siblings, cousins, aunts, uncles, or friends.

What happens at the table is very special. Our defenses melt away. The walls come down and our true selves show up. At the table we allow others to speak into our lives, and we have the privilege of speaking into theirs.

My grandfather's recipe for molasses cookies is one of my favorites. He was a farmer in northern Maine and one of the best bakers I've ever known. He spent the winter months as the head baker for the old Bellview Biltmore Resort Hotel in Dunedin, Florida. There's nothing like a big cup of tea and one of my grandpa's molasses cookies.

Grandpa's Molasses Cookies

1 cup molasses
1 cup brown sugar
1 cup shortening, margarine, or ½ butter
** & ½ lard**
2 eggs, beaten
2 tsp. vinegar
2 tsp. soda dissolved in 2 T water
5 cups flour
1 tsp. salt
2 tsp. ginger
½ tsp. cloves

Sift together dry ingredients. Mix wet and dry ingredients together, and let stand in a bowl in the refrigerator overnight, or at least a couple of hours until well chilled. Roll out and cut ¾-inch thick. Bake at 400° about 8–10 minutes.

SONDRA McCARTY
production assistant
WRMB—Boynton Beach, Florida

I am the production assistant for "Mornings" with Audrey here at WRMB, and of course an avid listener of Midday Connection.

The following recipe for Friendship Pie *is a staple dessert at all WRMB functions; if I don't take it, I'm not allowed to participate in the party. The same applies to family functions, so it is easy for me to know what to bring. It is simple to prepare and makes either 2 9" pies or 3 8" pies. They keep in the freezer for 3–4 months, so you can always have one on hand for unexpected guests. It is fairly rich and definitely not heart-healthy, but it is delicious, and I think it's OK to treat ourselves once in a while. (Even those of us who have had quintuple bypass surgery!)*

Friendship Pie

1 stick margarine or butter
2 cups coconut
1 cup slivered almonds
1 can Eagle milk
1 8 oz. package cream cheese (room temperature)
1 16 oz. container Cool Whip
1 jar caramel or chocolate ice cream topping
   (your preference)
2 9-inch or 3 8-inch graham cracker crusts

Melt butter in 350° oven. In melted butter, toast coconut and almonds together. Stir after 10 minutes and cook another 2–3 minutes until golden brown. Drain and cool mixture on paper towel.

In a large mixing bowl combine canned milk and cream cheese. Beat until smooth. Fold in Cool Whip. Stir in ⅓ of the coconut/almond mixture. Divide mixture evenly into pie shells. Top with remaining coconut/almond mixture. Drizzle ice cream topping over the top and freeze at least 2 hours.

LORI NEFF
Midday Connection producer/administrator

These are my all-time favorite cookies. My grandma Febus made them for the grandchildren, so of course I think of her every time I make them. I remember sitting on the red chair that they kept especially for the grandkids eating these cookies that I only got at Grandma's. By the way, my husband and I don't like coconut, but we love it in these cookies!

Grandma's Cornflake Cookies

½ cup butter
½ cup sugar
½ cup brown sugar
1 egg
1 cup flour
1½ tsp. baking powder
¼ tsp. salt
1 cup coconut
1 cup cornflakes

Cream butter with sugars. Beat egg into mixture. Sift dry ingredients and beat creamed sugars into dry mixture. Stir in coconut and cornflakes. Drop by tablespoons 2" apart on ungreased cookie sheet. The cookies will really flatten out while they bake. Bake at 350° for 10 minutes.

NORMA PEDERSON
wife of Wayne Pederson, vice president of MBN

This cookie recipe is a favorite of Wayne's from his childhood. His mom died when he was in college, but we still make these cookies.

Oatmeal Cookies

½ cup butter
½ cup shortening
2 cups brown sugar
3 eggs
1 cup sour cream
2 tsp. baking soda
1 tsp. salt
4 cups flour
4 cups oatmeal
1 pkg. chocolate chips or 2 cups raisins

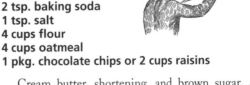

Cream butter, shortening, and brown sugar. Add eggs and sour cream. Mix dry ingredients and add in order given. Drop on cookie sheet and bake 8–10 minutes in 350° oven.

Amy Rios
executive assistant to MBN vice president

The following recipe was given to me by my best friend, Misty Porter. It's the best apple pie I have ever had and is really easy to make.

Misty's Apple Pie
1 deep-dish pie crust
4 small green apples (or 2 large)
2 tsp. cinnamon
3 T sugar
2–3 dashes allspice

Topping
1 cup sugar
¾ cup butter (melted)
1 cup flour (packed)
1 egg

Cut apples into small pieces and place in pie crust. Cover with cinnamon, sugar, and allspice. Set aside. Mix topping ingredients, making sure to pack the flour (this is key), until mixture resembles a thin cookie dough. Pour on top of apples and bake at 350° for 45 minutes to 1 hour. Enjoy!

 ## Melinda Schmidt
Midday Connection host

Coming to the table for a meal isn't worth much if there isn't something really good to eat waiting for you there. And I look forward to finishing off my day around the table with those I really want to talk and laugh with. I am into easy, homey recipes. I am not into fussy food. So I leave the Junior League Cookbook recipes to my friends who so creatively put them together, and I look for easy but yummy things to prepare!

At every evening meal, I've got a candle lit on the table. While Dave and I long for meals in Italy with family and friends gathered around a long table out in the vineyard, with pottery platters of good food, laughter, and a sort of meandering, hours-long, enriching mealtime . . . our family dinners more often have the feel of a circus that needs a referee!

The four of us are talkers, and there's way too much personality, daily stories, and drama for our own good. Surprisingly, we don't end the meal in heartburn, and I've never lost the desire to make something heartwarming for our dinner. And I'm always grateful that God has honored my request to bring us safely together at the end of another day.

I consider this pie-crust recipe to be a gift I can give you! It is so easy and I got it out of an American Heart Association cookbook a long time ago, so somehow that made it seem healthy! There's no excuse not to make a pie or quiche with this homemade crust—remember, I'm into easy! My in-laws always tell me I could win a county fair bake-off with this recipe, but I can't take much credit—I just follow the directions and out pops this delicious crust. Try it!

Mrs. Park's Pie Crust

Makes one 9-inch pie crust

1⅓ cup all-purpose flour
⅓ tsp. salt
⅓ cup oil
3 T water

Fill a measuring cup or small bowl with some water and ice cubes (you'll measure water out of this). Mix salt and flour in a bowl. Measure the vegetable oil in a liquid measure and add the measured ice water. Whisk together and then pour into flour mixture. Stir with a fork until blended into a ball. Roll dough between two sheets of waxed paper. (Sprinkle water on your countertop, place one sheet of waxed paper down on top of that, followed by dough and another piece of waxed paper. Now you're ready to roll it out!)

JANICE CARMODY
Oak Lawn, IL—WMBI

A coworker gave me this recipe thirteen years ago. As a young girl she escaped from Cuba to the USA, lying flat in a small boat across the night waters. I think of her every time I make this recipe (which is often).

Potato-Chip Cookies

Kid-friendly and adults love them.

2 sticks butter
2 sticks margarine (not low-fat)
1 cup sugar
2 egg yolks
3 cups flour
1½ cups crushed potato chips (regular chips)
2 tsp. vanilla
powdered sugar
optional: 1 cup chopped nuts

Soften butter and margarine, cream in sugar, add other ingredients, and mix till blended. Drop by teaspoons on baking sheet. Bake at 350° for 10 minutes, till brown on edges. Remove onto paper towel to cool, and sprinkle with sifted powdered sugar. Lick the powdered sugar from fingertips.

CARALYN CLARK
Indianapolis, IN—WGNR

This is a tasty twist on plain ol' oatmeal cookies! They are reasonably "heart-healthy"—with the oatmeal and fruit.

Fruity Oatmeal Cookies

1 cup butter, softened
1¾ cups brown sugar
2 eggs
1 T vanilla

2¼ cups all-purpose flour
1 cup quick cooking oats
1 tsp. baking soda
1 tsp. salt

Goodies

1 cup chocolate chips (or mini M&M's)
¾ cup Craisins (or raisins)
¾ cup coarsely chopped pecans (optional)

Cream together butter and sugar. Add eggs and vanilla. In separate bowl, combine dry ingredients. Blend dry ingredients into creamed mixture. Stir in goodies. Bake 10–12 minutes in a preheated 350° oven.

DIANE FAULKNER
Portage, IN—WMBI

Kids can help decorate this cake. It is healthy and I make this cake about every 1½ to 2 weeks for my family. They love it. Yes, this recipe is correct when I say to use olive oil—I use it in all my cakes. I never use cake mixes, so I don't know if that will work. Years ago, my grandfather was a chef on a train. He loved to cook and bake and so do I. This cake is very moist.

Extra-Moist Mocha Cake

2 cups all-purpose flour
1 tsp. salt
1 tsp. baking powder
2 tsp. baking soda
¾ cup baking cocoa (unsweetened)
2 cups sugar
1 cup hot brewed espresso coffee
1 cup plain olive oil (*not* extra virgin or light)
1 cup milk
2 eggs
1 tsp. vanilla (no imitation)

Mix all dry ingredients in a large mixing bowl. Add oil, coffee, and milk; mix at medium speed for 2 minutes. Add eggs and vanilla; beat 2 more minutes. Using the same olive oil, grease and flour a 9x13" cake pan or two 9-inch cake pans and pour the batter into the pans.

Bake at 350° for about 30 minutes, until the center springs back when touched. You may also insert a toothpick or knife. If it comes out clean, the cake is done. Let cool before frosting.

You can frost the cake using your favorite icing, Cool Whip, or stabilized whipped cream followed by a light dusting of sifted cocoa powder. Top with your favorite ice cream, or place a paper doily on top of the cake and using a sifter, sprinkle it with a mixture of powdered sugar and cocoa powder to make a pattern.

DEBORAH FRANSON
Normal, IL—WBNH

I got this recipe from my husband, Bruce's, mom years ago, because it's his favorite dessert. We have it for Thanksgiving and sometimes for Christmas too. We began the tradition of eating this dessert with Bruce's family for our holiday dessert years ago when they came here. In addition to his parents and sometimes his sister and her family coming, for two years we had foreign exchange students, one from Japan and one from China, share the Thanksgiving feast with us.

Chocolate Graham Cracker Delight

1 6 oz. package semisweet chocolate bits
½ cup light corn syrup
2 T water (or a bit more)
1 cup heavy cream, whipped
1 tsp. vanilla
20 graham crackers

Melt chocolate bits over hot, not boiling, water. Remove from water, and stir in syrup and water until smooth. Reserve ¼ cup of this chocolate mixture to use as glaze. Add vanilla to cream; whip. Fold the whipped cream and vanilla into remainder of chocolate mixture. Place 5 graham crackers, broken into large pieces, in bottom of waxed-paper-lined 10x5x3" pan. Pour ⅓ filling over crackers. Repeat to get 4 cracker layers and 3 filling layers. Drizzle glaze over top. While the glaze has been set aside, it may thicken too much to be of drizzling consistency, so you may have to stir in a drop or two of water to thin it enough to drizzle on top. Freeze until glaze is firm. Wrap and freeze. Serve with waxed paper removed. Slice lengthwise in half, then crosswise into 2-inch slices. Eat and enjoy!

ANNETTE FORE
(ANITA LUSTREA'S MOTHER)
Sarasota, FL—WKZM

This Christmas tradition is special to me because it involved the whole family. I baked and frosted while the family decorated. The last sheet of cookies would be personalized, each one with the person's name on it, and we got to eat our own right away. What a great time of singing and laughing with sugar and decorations all over the table and sometimes even the floor. Memories! Memories!

Butter Cookies

1 cup butter
½ cup sugar
1 egg
½ tsp. almond flavoring
2½ cups sifted flour

Cream butter and sugar until fluffy Add egg and almond flavoring, and beat well. Gradually add flour. Chill for at least 1 hour in the refrigerator. Roll out on floured board fairly thin. Cut with cookie cutters in traditional Christmas shapes. Bake at 350° until color appears around the edges. Remove, cool, and decorate. Enjoy!

LYNETTE HERSHBERGER
Dalton, OH—WCRF

This recipe is quick. Kids can help to make it and love to eat it. It's good for kids of all ages! My kids always love to stir the red hots until they melt. I would consider it inexpensive also, and I nearly always have the ingredients on hand.

Cinnamon Applesauce Jell-O

2 cups water
¼ cup red hot candies
2–3 oz. cherry Jell-O
3 cups applesauce (unsweetened is best)

Bring two cups of water to a boil. Add the red hots and stir until candy is melted. Then add Jell-O and stir until dissolved. Now stir in the applesauce (in place of the cold liquid). Pour into a bowl and place in the refrigerator until set. (Could put in separate small serving bowls if you wish.) This will add a pretty red color and appealing flavor and texture to your meal.

STEPHANIE GLOVER

Euclid, OH—WCRF

I've made this recipe almost every year for Thanksgiving for about the last ten years. My aunt Vernetta (who turned seventy this year) adapted it from a recipe from her father, my grandfather, who was born in 1901 and died in 1979. The recipe yields 2 9-inch pies. (I use the packaged frozen pie crusts, which need to unthaw for about 20 minutes.)

Aunt V's Sweet Potato Pie

6 medium sweet potatoes or yams
4 eggs
1½ sticks of butter (softened)
3 cups sugar
¼ cup milk
2 tsp. cinnamon
2 tsp. nutmeg
2 tsp. vanilla extract
1 pinch salt

Boil washed whole sweet potatoes (with the skin on) 30–35 minutes until able to pierce with a fork. Allow to cool at least 20 minutes. Preheat oven to 350°. Peel skin off potatoes and cut up into small pieces. Add softened butter to warm potatoes and whip about 5 minutes until completely whipped. If potatoes are stringy or lumpy, strain with a strainer. Add sugar, eggs, and milk and beat about 2 minutes. Add all other ingredients and beat 1 minute. Pour into unthawed pie crusts and bake for 50–55 minutes until knife inserted in middle comes out clean.

HEATHER HARRISON

Fort Stewart, GA—WBBN

This is a recipe that my granny made. Granny was the rock in our family. Since she went home to the Lord, this has been a comforting reminder of her. This is a kid-friendly, quick, and inexpensive recipe.

Peach Cobbler

1 (15 oz.) can of peaches
1 cup self-rising flour
1 cup sugar
1 cup milk
1 stick butter

Open and drain can of peaches. In a mixing bowl combine flour, sugar, and milk. In a large loaf pan or 8x8" pan, melt the stick of butter in oven. When butter is melted, add the flour mixture to pan. Do not mix. Then add peaches, but do not mix. Bake in a 400° oven until bubbly and golden brown. Enjoy with vanilla ice cream.

SABRA INGEMAN

Tequesta, FL—WRMB

These soft cookies get compliments everywhere I take them. My kids and husband love them. I originally tried this recipe because it contains molasses, an old-fashioned ingredient that reminds me of my grandmother. She always had a jar in her kitchen. She told me that I had a beautiful body and to never harm it with "those bad drugs." She told me this during my ugly/awkward 10-year-old stage, which was also during the early 1970s psychedelic period. I never did try any of "those bad drugs." She died at age 94. Now I tell my children the same thing!

Cinnamon Snaps

¾ cup softened butter
¾ cup packed brown sugar
1 egg
⅓ cup molasses
2¼ cups all-purpose flour
2 tsp. baking soda
2 tsp. ground cinnamon
½ tsp. salt
Additional granulated white sugar

Cream butter and brown sugar together. Add egg and molasses. Mix well. Add remaining ingredients gradually (except white sugar). Refrigerate dough for a few minutes until dough can be rolled into 1-inch balls. Make balls and then roll each ball in the white sugar until covered.

Place 2 inches apart on ungreased cookie sheet. Bake at 350° for about 12 minutes or until tops of cookies crack. Remove cookies from oven and cool for 30 seconds, and then carefully remove to wire racks and continue to cool. Once completely cooled, store in an airtight container. Cookies stay soft and delicious for about one week.

CHRISTINE JOHNSON
Salem, WI—WMBI

Quick, kid-friendly, and heart-healthy. I love to serve my family this dessert. They think it is an indulgent, rich treat, but I secretly know it is healthy for them. It is made with dark chocolate and my secret ingredient, tofu.

Tofu Chocolate Pie
Makes 8 servings

2 cups dark chocolate morsels
⅓ cup coffee liqueur
1 tsp. vanilla extract
1 block soft silken tofu
1 T honey
1 9-inch prepared graham cracker crust

Melt chocolate morsels and coffee liqueur in double boiler over medium heat. Stir in vanilla.

Combine tofu, chocolate mixture, and honey in blender. Blend until smooth.

Pour the filling into the crust and refrigerate at least 2 hours until the filling is set.

ROXIE LYONS
Chattanooga, TN—WMBW

This delicious drink has helped me lose weight. It helps curb my appetite. It is a great between-meals snack. For those in Weight Watchers, it only contains 3 points, or in Nutri-System, it serves as a snack (1 dairy, 1 fruit). Heart-healthy, quick, inexpensive, fat-free, low calories, very filling and satisfying.

Fruit Smoothie

1 small package Jell-O sugar-free
/fat-free Instant Pudding (any
flavor, but cheesecake makes
a great combo with most fruit)
1 cup fruit, fresh, frozen, or canned
(lite syrup or in its own juices)
1 cup skim milk
1 cup ice (If you use frozen fruit, you won't
need the ice)

In a blender, liquefy the milk and fruit. Add the Jell-O and blend. Add the ice.

Mix all ingredients together in blender until ice or frozen fruit is totally crushed.

PHYLLIS MCDANIEL
Madisonville, TN—WMBW

I have made this recipe for my children, grandchildren, and many more children, who have all loved it. They say it makes them feel special, and they remember it because they helped with it. Also they have passed it on by making it with children. It can be made with many flavors and topped with Cool Whip or icing, with sprinkles—or just use your imagination. This is also inexpensive, great for birthdays, church suppers, bake sales, etc.

Ice-Cream Cone Cakes
Makes 24

1 package cake mix
24 flat bottom ice-cream cones
1 tub ready-made frosting (any flavor)
any kind of sprinkles, chocolate chips,
   coconut, colored sugars, etc.

Heat oven to 350º. Place paper baking cup in each of 24 muffin cups. Make cake mix as directed on package, using water, oil, and eggs. Fill each muffin cup ⅔ full of batter (2 heaping tablespoons each). Place ice-cream cone upside down on batter in each cup. Bake 20 minutes (cones may tilt on batter). Cool in pan 10 minutes. Remove from pan to wire rack. Cool completely, about 30 minutes. Remove paper baking cups. Frost cupcakes with frosting; decorate with decors.

DOUG MILLER

Cleveland, OH—WCRF

This recipe was from a warm, receptive, kind neighbor friend's mom. This family is very dear to me and was always there for me whenever I needed them. This is my favorite dessert, and I loved the name because I was a big sports fan when I was young.

O'Henry Bars

⅔ cup margarine
1 cup brown sugar
½ cup white corn syrup
1 T vanilla
4 cups quick cooking oats
6 oz. milk chocolate chips
⅔ cup crunchy peanut butter

Cream butter and sugar. Add syrup, vanilla, and oats. Spread evenly across a greased square pan. Bake at 350° for 15 minutes, then let cool.

Meanwhile, melt chocolate chips and peanut butter in a double boiler over medium-high heat till it melts only (not boiling). Spread topping over bars. Then let cool for about ½ hour, cut, and serve.

BEVERLY NAY

Camby, IN—WGNR

This recipe was given to me by my cousin at the 2006 annual "Confer Family Reunion" in Monroe, Indiana. Four generations of family members travel from Michigan, Illinois, Florida, and many locations in Indiana to share great food and renew family friendships each summer.

This is a quick mocha dessert treat!

Mocha Brownie Dessert

cooled 9x13" pan of brownies
1 T and 1 tsp. instant coffee
¼ cup hot water
2 boxes instant white chocolate pudding
milk
12 oz. Cool Whip
toffee bits

Crumble brownies in a large bowl. Mix coffee and hot water in a 2-cup measuring cup. Fill the measuring cup up to the 2-cup line with milk. Mix this milk mixture with the pudding mixes. Fold Cool Whip into the pudding mixture. Layer the brownies and the pudding mixture in a pretty serving bowl. Sprinkle the top layer with toffee bits. Refrigerate. M-m-m, this is so-o good! Enjoy this creamy chocolate dessert with your favorite beverage.

DEBI OWINYO

Bonners Ferry, ID—KMBI

*This cake is super easy and quick, yet tastes **wonderful** and is made-from-scratch. It even has nutritive value with the large amount of rhubarb. This is the kind of dessert you would make if you forgot it was your turn to take treats to church or for a potluck when you have no time to cook! This is quick and inexpensive if you have access to home-grown rhubarb.*

Rhubarb Custard Cake

1 package (for 13x9" pan) yellow cake mix
4 cups chopped fresh or frozen rhubarb
1 cup sugar
1 cup whipping cream (or evaporated milk)
optional: whipped cream and fresh mint

Prepare batter according to package directions. Pour into greased 13x9" baking dish. Sprinkle with rhubarb and sugar. Slowly pour cream over top. Do not stir! Bake at 350° for 40–45 minutes or until golden brown. Cool 15 minutes before serving. Garnish with whipped cream and mint, if desired.

LYNDA PHILLIPS
North Aurora, IL—WMBI

This cake was a favorite that my late aunt Sarrah made whenever she had company over. It is quick, inexpensive, and very easy to make.

Aunt Sarrah's Chocolate Cherry Cake

1 pkg. chocolate fudge cake mix
2 eggs
1 tsp. almond extract
1 can cherry pie filling*

Preheat oven to 350°. Mix together and spread in a greased 13x9" cake pan. Bake at 350° for 20 minutes.

Frosting

1 cup sugar
⅓ cup milk
⅓ cup butter
1 cup semisweet chocolate chips

In saucepan, combine sugar, milk, and butter. Cook until sugar is dissolved and butter is melted. Remove pan from heat. Stir in chocolate chips until melted. Pour over warm cake. Store cake in refrigerator. This is a very moist cake without the oil.

* *I have used other pie fillings with other cake mixes.*

MARCIA PAULEY
East Peoria, IL—WBNH

Chocolate Peanut Butter Bars

1½ cups packed brown sugar
2 sticks of butter or 1 cup Smart Balance regular spread
½ tsp. vanilla
4 cups old-fashioned oats
1 (6 oz.) package of chocolate chips
1 cup smooth or chunky natural peanut butter

Cream together sugar and butter. Add vanilla. Stir in oatmeal; mix thoroughly. Pat into an 11x15" baking sheet. Bake 15–20 minutes at 375°. While this is baking, melt chocolate chips and peanut butter in top of double boiler. When melted and mixed together, spread over baked bars. When cool, cut into squares. Keep refrigerated.

Linda Raber
Plain City, OH—WEEC

This family favorite recipe takes me back to my childhood in the 1950s and "baking day" with my mother. Saturdays we prepared baked goods for the upcoming week, a tradition I continue.

Cheese Custard Pie

1 9" unbaked pie shell
8 oz. cream cheese, cut into 6–8 pieces
2 eggs, separated
1 cup evaporated milk
¾ cup whole milk
¾ cup sugar
2 T flour
½ tsp. vanilla
pinch of salt

Preheat oven to 400°. Place cream cheese, egg yolks, milks, sugar, flour, vanilla, and salt in blender. Blend until smooth and pour into large mixing bowl.

In a medium bowl beat egg whites until semi-stiff. Fold into milk/cream cheese mixture. Pour into a 9" unbaked pie crust. Bake at 400° for 15 minutes. Reduce heat to 375°, and bake an additional 15 minutes. Reduce heat to 325°, and bake for additional 15 minutes. Remove from oven, cool, and enjoy!

Rita Ross (Lori Neff's Mom)
Delta, OH—WMBI over the internet

This was my grandma Victoria Bozarth's ("Grandma Bo") favorite chocolate cake recipe. Grandma was a terrific cook who didn't need a recipe to cook, patterns to sew, or instructions on how to love her grandchildren.

Grandma's Chocolate Cake

3 cups flour
2 cups sugar
½ cup cocoa
1 tsp. salt
2 tsp. baking soda
2 eggs
1 cup shortening
1 cup hot water
1 cup sour milk
2 tsp. vanilla

Mix all ingredients together and bake at 350° for 35 minutes.

Christina Rutzebeck
Homer, AK—Internet listener

This was my mom's recipe that my dad used in his restaurant. He loved to bake, and I watched with much anticipation as he made huge batches of these cookies. As a child I ate these cookies all the time as our apartment was on top of the restaurant. They were very famous in our small Alaska town. I now use the recipe for any and all occasions, and make them with my kids. Everyone raves about them. My dad is now deceased and I love remembering him this way.

This recipe is quick, kid-friendly, inexpensive, and easy to make.

Oatmeal/Chocolate Chip Cookies

3 cups flour
2 tsp. baking soda
2 tsp. salt
1 cup shortening (butter flavor works best)
1 cup butter
1½ cup brown sugar
1½ cup granulated sugar
2 tsp. vanilla
2 tsp. water
4 eggs
4 cups oats
½–2 cups chocolate chips

Heat oven to 375°. Mix flour, soda, and salt. Set aside. Blend shortening, butter, sugars, vanilla, and water. Beat in eggs. Add flour mixture, and mix well. Stir in oats and chocolate chips. Drop by rounded ½ teaspoonfuls on cookie sheet. (I personally like them bigger, but you have to make sure they get cooked long enough.) Bake at 375° for 11 minutes.

BRENDA SCHEETZ
Alamogordo, NM—Internet listener

This is my mother, Norma Scheetz's, recipe. She used to make this for me so I could take it back to school with me. Since I was rarely home and had to go away to school, as a totally blind child, she knew this recipe, Texas Sheet Cake, comforted me. Now Mom is dying of cancer, and I'd love to put this in your book in memory of Norma Scheetz, of Follansbee, WV.

Texas Sheet Cake

2 sticks margarine
1 cup water
¼ cup cocoa
2 cups flour
½ tsp. salt
2 cups white sugar
1 tsp. baking soda
2 beaten eggs
½ cup sour cream

Combine margarine, water, and cocoa in a saucepan. Add additional ingredients. Bring to a boil and remove from heat. Mix together and bake in a large slab cake pan (17x11" pan) at 350° for 22 minutes. Note: You can bake this on a cookie sheet with sides.

Icing

1 stick butter
1 tsp. vanilla
6 T milk
¼ cup cocoa
1 box powdered sugar

Heat butter until it is melted. Add other ingredients, and stir. Add nuts if desired.

RALYN SNYDER
Springfield, OH—WEEC

I chose this one because it is extremely easy, fairly inexpensive, and always a huge hit when I take it anywhere. My cousin brought a plate of these cheesecake squares to my family when my grandmother passed away. To this day, my cousins and I hold Donna (the originator—at least to our family—of this recipe) in high esteem. I encouraged my younger cousins—one at a time—to sneak out to my car during the funeral visiting hours to try one. They were not disappointed.

Cinnamon Cheesecake Squares

2 cans of crescent rolls
2 8 oz. packages of cream cheese (reduced fat works too, but not fat free)
1 cup sugar
1 tsp. vanilla
margarine or spray butter
sugared cinnamon

Grease the bottom of a 13x9" pan (a deep cookie sheet can also be used). Unroll 1 can of crescent rolls in the bottom of the pan and press into the corners. In a separate bowl, place cream cheese (softened), sugar, and vanilla. Whip together with whisk or wooden spoon. Spread mixture over crescent rolls. Top with remaining can of crescent rolls. Pour melted butter on top, or spray butter works very well. Sprinkle generously with a cinnamon sugar mix. Bake at 350° for 20–25 minutes or until top is browned. Allow to cool. I usually chill it for a couple of hours before I cut it into pieces. Great for your next potluck!

MINDY URQUHART
Guys Mills, PA—WCRF

I love this recipe for a couple of reasons—one, it's quick, easy, and inexpensive, as well as low in fat! Two, because my family loves it—it feels like indulging in a special treat on a holiday even though it's very simple to make.

Chocolate-Covered Cherry Cake

1 box of devil's food cake mix
1 can of cherry pie filling

Mix the two ingredients together until well blended. *Do not* add the remaining ingredients called for on the box. Bake as the box indicates. That's it! It makes a wonderfully moist and delicious cake that tastes like having a chocolate-covered cherry. I hope you enjoy!

KAREN VAN NOSTRAN
Youngstown, OH—WCRF-FM

I have taken this to families who have lost a loved one as it is good warm or the next day. It is easy and delicious, and your whole house smells great when you bake it.

Graham Streusel Coffee Cake

Topping

¾ cup butter (not margarine), melted
¾ cup brown sugar, packed
1½ tsp. cinnamon
1 cup walnuts, coarsely chopped
1 pkg. graham crackers (⅓ of 16 oz. box), finely crushed

Mix together and set aside.

Cake

1 box super-moist yellow cake mix
1 cup water
⅓ cup oil
3 eggs

Mix cake as directed on box, using above ingredients. Pour half of the batter into a 9x13" greased and floured pan. Sprinkle ½ the topping over batter. Pour remaining batter in pan and add remaining topping. Bake at 350° for 40 to 45 minutes (until toothpick comes out clean). This is wonderful served warm or cold.

LAURA WILSON
Kettle Falls, WA—KMBI

*This recipe was my great-grandmother Nanny Long's, cake. This was and still is the first item for the children in our family to learn how to cook. It has been passed down now for five, going on six, generations. There are so many happy memories attached to the "building" (as my daughter used to say) of this cake! I have modified it to being heart-healthy by substituting whole wheat flour and Splenda or **natural/raw** sugar (but don't tell Nanny Long!).*

Three-Holer Cake

1½ cups flour
1 cup sugar
¼ cup baking cocoa
1 tsp. baking soda
½ tsp. salt
1 tsp. vanilla
1 tsp. vinegar
⅓ cup oil
1 cup water

Sift all of the dry ingredients together 3 times and place in an 8x8" pan. Combine vanilla, vinegar, and oil. Make three holes in the dry ingredients, and in these holes place the liquid. Then pour water over all. Mix thoroughly and place in a 350° oven for about 35 minutes. (You know it is ready when you lightly push in the center and it springs back.)

It is perfect without frosting, but you can add a squirt of whipped cream on top of each serving to make it pretty!

CHERI YOUNG
Chattaroy, WA—KMBI

This recipe was passed on to me by my mother-in-law many years ago. She was a superb cook and the best apple-pie maker. This cookie is great anytime and easy to make. The touch of orange with chocolate is an interesting combination.

Frosted Orange Chippers

Cookies

1 cup softened margarine or butter
1 3 oz. pkg. cream cheese, softened
1 cup sugar
1 tsp. vanilla
1 T grated orange rind
2 eggs
2 cups sifted flour
1 tsp. salt
1 6 oz. package chocolate chips

Cream together margarine, cream cheese, and sugar until light and fluffy. Stir in vanilla and orange rind. Add eggs one at a time, beating well after each addition. Sift flour and salt, and stir into creamed mixture. Add chocolate chips. Drop by teaspoonfuls onto greased cookie sheet. Bake at 350° for about 10 minutes or until lightly browned. While warm, frost with orange frosting. (See below.)

Orange Frosting

2 cups powdered sugar
4 tsp. margarine
2½ T orange juice, or enough to make mixture
    thin enough to paint on cookie
¼ tsp. grated orange rind
dash of salt

Blend well. Tint with a few drops of orange food coloring if desired. Use a small pastry brush to brush onto cookies.

A Full Meal

NEIL ATKINSON
author of The Shrewd Christian
www.theshrewdchristian.com

Called to Relationship

"Look at me. I stand at the door. I knock.
If you hear me call and open the door, I'll come right in and sit down to supper with you."
(REV. 3:20 THE MESSAGE)

A very wise man once said, "The Kingdom of God is the Kingdom of Right Relationships." I wish I was smart enough to have said that; its truth is simple but very powerful.

Consider: If the world is ours, but we have no friends (including family members), then life, at its most essential, is poor. Yet if the world is closing in on us in detrimental ways, but we have friends, especially family members, then life is rich.

Relationships are what life is about, and sharing a meal together is one of the great ways to develop relationships. Revelation 3:20 helps us to understand that truth; it is one of the great verses used by countless ministers in countless ways to point out that Jesus wants a relationship with us. And the verse uses a meal to describe the intimacy of the relationship.

Margie and I find that we have guests for dinner for two main reasons: ministry or fellowship. Sometimes people desperately need to be heard; dinner together is a perfect means to hear their story and meet their needs, that is, ministry. Sometimes we want to get to know people at a deeper level because we feel a great connection that enables our faith to grow, that is, fellowship.

Going out for dinner, while it can be quite good for either ministry or fellowship, is not as good as dinner in your home.

Four reasons for that:

1. The setting of a home is much more intimate than any restaurant,

2. the cost of a meal at home is less, much less, than that in a restaurant,

3. a server is not constantly interrupting good conversation with inane comments/questions ("Is everything wonderful?" "Enjoy"), and, finally,

4. the food is not as good at a restaurant as it is in a home.

The following menu is meant to help you focus on the reason for entertaining: ministry and/or fellowship. Although the meal will have higher than average cost, the results will be exceptionally higher than average. In other words, you will enjoy a much greater reward than that which is provided by a normal meal.

Bon appetit!

Dinner for Six
for Less than $35

First Course: Tapas

*Tapas, for the understanding of **nonrestaurant** owners, is a Spanish word that means "small bites." Tapas, for the understanding of **restaurant** owners, is a Spanish word that means "an extraordinarily small amount of food for an extraordinarily large price."*

Menu
Sweet/Fiery Things
Pumped-Up Mushrooms
Easy and Good Shrimp (from here on known as E/G Shrimp)
Beverages: whatever you like and think will work with the Tapas.

Ingredients
24 Wheat Thins (Tomato Basil Flavor)
Cream Cheese
Raspberry Chipotle BBQ Sauce
1 bunch of cilantro . . . no, parsley will not do the same thing . . . cilantro! (You also will be using cilantro in the entrée section.)
18 fresh mushrooms (Gaps should not be visible between stem and top.)
store-bought pesto OR make your own cilantro pesto—brings down the house!
18 frozen *uncooked* shrimp (26–30 count, meaning 26–30 shrimp per pound). Do not buy already cooked shrimp; they are tasteless and tough.

Preparation

Hours ahead of time

1. Search (diligently) for 6 attractive small plates and 6 attractive napkins. Warning: Do *not* buy any of these things as that will blow the budget. Search; they are there, but they are in hiding.

2. Coat each Wheat Thin with cream cheese and dab with raspberry chipotle BBQ sauce. If you are an enthusiastic person, go easy on the raspberry dab; if you are a reticent person, go heavy on the sauce. Top with one leaf of cilantro. Cover and chill in the refrigerator.

3. Stem the mushrooms and save the stems for making broth or flavoring any sauce. (See Stuffing recipe in Entrée section.) Spoon 1 tablespoon Pesto into mushroom cavity; spray baking sheet, put mushrooms on baking sheet, cover, and put in refrigerator.

4. Thaw, peel, and dry shrimp. Cover and put in refrigerator.

5. Put stick of butter in small pitcher . . . set close to microwave.

30 minutes before guests arrive

1. Heat oven to 400°.

2. Set Sweet/Fiery Things on the counter and allow to come to room temp.

3. Ditto Stuffed Mushrooms.

4. Ditto Shrimp.

5. While you heat nonstick skillet over medium-high heat, season the shrimp with salt and pepper and anything else you think might be good . . . but remember, butter is coming!

6. Assemble small plates near range.

7. Ditto beverage glasses.

10 minutes before guests arrive

1. Put ice and/or beverage in glasses.

2. Place 4 Sweet/Fiery Things on each plate.

3. Stick Stuffed Mushrooms in the oven.

4. Melt butter in microwave.

5. Spray high-heat cooking oil in skillet and pop in the E/G Shrimp. Caution: You now have *only* 2 or 3 minutes before the shrimp are done. Do *not* let them overcook.

As guests arrive

1. Have spouse greet them, or, if by yourself, yell for them to enter.

2. Put 3 E/G Shrimp on each plate.

3. Ditto 3 Mushrooms.

4. Lightly pour a bit of butter on the mushrooms and the shrimp.

5. Have each person grab a plate plus beverage and head for the living/family room.

6. Party.

7. Smile humbly and receive the compliments graciously.

Second Course:

Red Leaf Lettuce with Parmesan Crisps and Balsamic Vinaigrette

Heat oven to 400°.

6–8 oz. grated Parmesan cheese (grate it yourself; pre-grated will not work)
1 head of Red Leaf lettuce
2 oz. extra virgin olive oil (EVOO)
1 oz. balsamic vinegar
salt
pepper

Wash the lettuce, dry, tear into small pieces, and pile torn pieces on a salad plate. Refrigerate.

Combine EVOO with vinegar, and salt and pepper to taste. If you want to add Worchestershire sauce, I promise not to be offended. Refrigerate.

Use a nonstick baking sheet (or lightly spray regular baking sheet). Spread Parmesan evenly over cookie sheet and place in oven. After 6 minutes, watch closely. When brown edges creep toward the middle, remove from oven and place on cutting board. Use a pizza roller to cut the crisps into shapes that you think are attractive. Or, if you want to be extra creative, drape the cut, warm pieces over small glasses to give them a different shape.

When it is time to serve, drizzle the vinaigrette over the lettuce, arrange the crisps, and smile.

Entrée

It is my opinion that a true test of a chef/cook is how he/she can prepare a roast chicken. This most simple of all meals can easily suffer from over- under-done skins as well as dried out meat, and result in a mediocre experience. Mediocre is not excellent; simple is not necessarily easy.

The highlight of my culinary experience occurred when we entertained the chef/owner of one of the best restaurants in the state of Colorado at our home. I served the following recipe, and as Dominique took his first bite his face lit up and he said, "This is excellent!" I am still smiling at the memory.

It is your turn to create a smiling memory.

If you are new to cooking, follow the following recipes to the letter. If you are an experienced cook and want to lighten the meal by reducing/eliminating the butter, I will not track you down. Either way, you might want to practice the chicken dish on your family before you entertain your friends. Otherwise, live dangerously!

Menu

Roast Chicken with Cilantro and Garlic/Lemon
   Pan Juices
Mushroom Stuffing (no mushrooms required!)
Mashed/Pureed Gruyere Butternut Squash

Heat oven to 350°.

Mashed/Pureed Gruyere Butternut Squash

1 large butternut squash
4–6 oz. Gruyere cheese, shredded
2 T butter
salt
pepper

Cut squash in half (retain the seeds at this time, as it helps improve the flavor). Salt and pepper the cut side, place in glass casserole that contains ½ inch of water, and microwave until tender (15–20 minutes). Working quickly, remove the seeds, skin the squash, cut into pieces, and add the cheese and butter. If you want a rustic squash, use a potato to combine the ingredients. If you want a smooth concoction, use your food processor. Taste for seasoning. If needed, add more salt and/or pepper. Keep warm.

Mushroom Stuffing

1 package of Stove Top stuffing
1 qt. mushroom broth (*not* cream of mushroom
   soup . . . this is not your mother's recipe)

If you cannot find mushroom broth, dice the leftover stems of the mushrooms from the Tapas section, bring to a boil, reduce heat to low, and let the mixture steep for several minutes.

Roast Chicken with Cilantro and Garlic/Lemon Pan Juices

1 chicken, 3–4 lbs.
1 lemon
1 head of garlic
1 bunch of cilantro
½ stick of butter, softened to room temperature
salt
pepper

Trim chicken of extra fat and skin; wash and pat dry. (If you have the time, let the chicken sit in the refrigerator up to 24 hours; that time creates wonderfully crisp skin.)

Trim skin from each garlic clove. (If you are using late-season garlic, remove the middle green stem as this is a very bitter part of the garlic.) Stuff garlic in cavity.

Puncture lemon 10–15 times with a fork and place in cavity. Close cavity with toothpicks, grilling spears, or whatever.

Chop 3–5 T of cilantro and combine with the butter. Gently lift the breast skin of the chicken and slide the mixture under the skin, spreading it evenly over the breast. Do the same for the legs. Coat the skin with extra virgin olive oil, and season briskly with salt and pepper.

Empty package of Stove Top stuffing into the bottom of a small roasting pan. Pour 1½–2 cups mushroom/chicken broth over the stuffing.

Place an oiled rack over the stuffing, and put the chicken on it breast side down. Cook for 20 minutes; flip the chicken so the breast side is up, cook for another 25 minutes; increase the heat to 400°.

Add another cup of broth to the stuffing. Cook for another 20-40 minutes (yes, that long . . . your oven temperature may not be accurate and you may live at a funny altitude). Internal temp should be 165-170°, and the leg should move easily and produce clear juices. (If the chicken skin looks as if it is burning before the chicken is done, place a piece of foil over it.)

Bring the chicken to a cutting board, tilt it, and pour juices, garlic, and lemon into a small saucepan; cover the chicken gently with foil and let rest.

For the pan juices, mash garlic, squeeze lemon, and add ¼ cup of liquid: stock, wine, etc. Bring to a boil, strain, discard solids, and taste for possible seasoning adjustment. Put back on heat and reduce by half. (Reduce by half means that you must boil it until half has evaporated.)

To Plate

1. Carve chicken.

2. Place one serving of stuffing in the center of each plate.

3. Divide one serving of squash and place on either side of stuffing.

4. Place one serving of chicken in center of stuffing.

5. Drizzle pan juices over the chicken.

6. Garnish with cilantro and serve.

7. Smile.

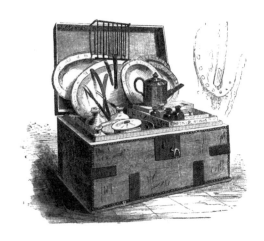

Final Course: Dessert

Chocolate/Raspberry Creamed Death

½ gallon premium vanilla ice cream
1 pint fresh raspberries
½ cup Hershey's chocolate sauce
2–3 T butter softened to room temperature
1 T sugar

Place 1 or 2 scoops of ice cream into 9 dessert bowls. Return to freezer.

Heat chocolate sauce in microwave, add butter, combine, heat again. Should taste extra rich. If necessary, add more butter.

In a nonstick skillet, add raspberries and sprinkle with sugar. Heat until the raspberries give off their juices.

Bring out 6 ice cream servings; add most (but not all) of the raspberries, drizzle a sizable amount of the chocolate sauce (but not all), and serve immediately.

When someone asks for seconds, bring out the other 3 bowls, and pour on the reserved raspberries and chocolate (well, if you want to use both of these, go right ahead).

Berry Gratin

(from Sally Schneider, bless her)

½ pint blackberries or raspberries
½ cup sour cream
4 T brown sugar

Turn on the broiler and make sure a shelf is appropriately placed 3-4" under the broiler.

Put berries in large shallow bowl.

Stir sour cream to liquefy it slightly and pour over berries. Sieve (push through a strainer) brown sugar over berries. Put the bowl under the broiler until the sugar bubbles and begins to caramelize. Don't burn it. Serve at once.

Be sure to have your most winning smile available; it will be needed.

Index of Contributors

Index of Recipes

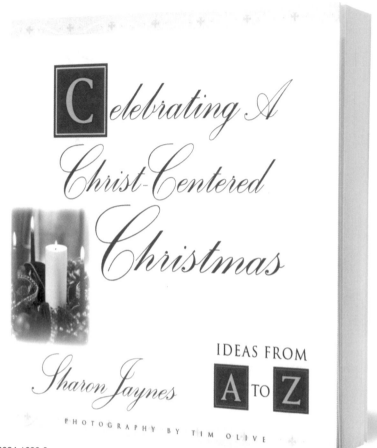

ISBN-10: 0-8024-1699-3
ISBN-13: 978-0-8024-1699-5

Christ has been crowded out of Christmas by shopping malls, parties, and decorations. Sharon Jaynes offers help to return our focus to the baby in the manger. Organized A to Z, Celebrating a Christ-Centered Christmas is filled with twenty-six innovative and creative ways to do just that. Come let your focus be renewed and use these great ideas to have a joyous celebration of the Savior's birth.

by Sharon Jaynes
Find it now at your favorite local or online bookstore.
www.MoodyPublishers.com
www.WomenRise.com

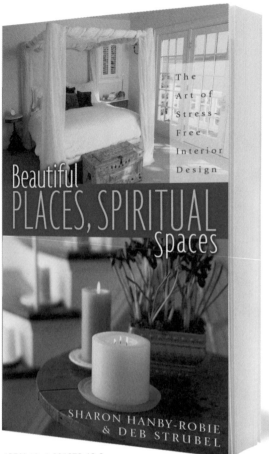

ISBN-10: 1-881273-18-0
ISBN-13: 978-1-881273-18-9

Today's fast pace allows little room for time-consuming trips to decorating stores. Or perhaps the lack of funds keeps us from furnishing and redecorating our homes. This is a Bible study to understand how to build and maintain a biblical atmosphere in our homes. Designed to meet the needs of today's woman, *Beautiful Places, Spiritual Spaces* is the ideal companion for women navigating the uncharted territory of life - offering daily, short, inspirational mediations, and creative decorating how-to's.

by Sharon Hanby-Robie and Deb Strubel
Find it now at your favorite local or online bookstore.

www.MoodyPublishers.com

www.WomenRise.com

MBN *Midday Connection*

Moody Broadcasting Network
A Ministry of Moody Bible Institute

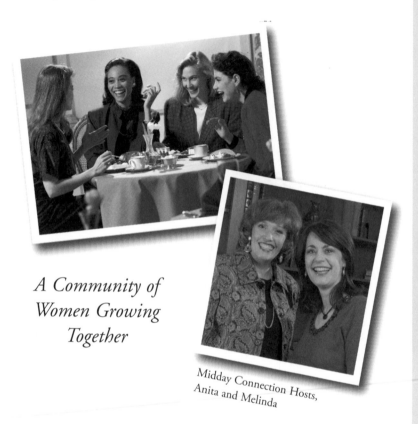

*A Community of
Women Growing
Together*

Midday Connection Hosts,
Anita and Melinda

ANITA LUSTREA and **MELINDA SCHMIDT** are two moms who also happen to be radio talk show hosts of Moody Broadcasting's *Midday Connection*, a call-in talk program for women. Each day thousands of women across the country tune in to be encouraged, challenged and inspired to go deeper in their walk with Christ and to live full lives that honor God. Anita and Melinda are seasoned radio veterans whose passion for women spills out each day on the air.

Join us every weekday at noon CST, and participate
in the program - by phone or email!

312. 329. 4460 | midday@moody.edu

www.MiddayConnection.org

How many of you love to sit down with a friend over a cup of coffee? At *Midday Connection* we do that every weekday with a whole host of friends, both nationally recognized guests and listeners who are looking for unique daily dialog that touches their hearts. *Midday Connection* is a radio program geared primarily toward women, and it's filled with encouragement that focuses on growing the whole person: body, mind and soul. During this live one hour radio show, hosted by Anita Lustrea and Melinda Schmidt, phone lines light up with listener questions and comments coast-to-coast. It's our goal to bring to those listeners relevant content about issues that really matter: issues like marriage, parenting, the workplace, finances, and one's spiritual life.

We see *Midday Connection* as a community of women growing together, and we hope you'll become a part of that community. In the midst of your busy life, we hope *Midday Connection* will be that refreshing break in the middle of the day where you can connect with old and new friends. And where, as the end of Matthew chapter 28 reads, you can receive "rest for your souls."

Head to our website, www.middayconnection.org, for more information about *Midday Connection*, including our Book Club and audio archives.